William H. H. Kelke

A Digest of the Law of Practice

under the judicature acts and rules and the cases decided in the chancery

and common law divisions from November 1875 to August 1880

William H. H. Kelke

A Digest of the Law of Practice
under the judicature acts and rules and the cases decided in the chancery and common law divisions from November 1875 to August 1880

ISBN/EAN: 9783337158934

Printed in Europe, USA, Canada, Australia, Japan

Cover: Foto ©Suzi / pixelio.de

More available books at **www.hansebooks.com**

A DIGEST

OF THE

LAW OF PRACTICE

UNDER THE

JUDICATURE ACTS AND RULES,

AND THE

CASES DECIDED

IN THE CHANCERY AND COMMON LAW DIVISIONS,
FROM NOVEMBER, 1875, TO AUGUST, 1880.

BY

W. H. HASTINGS KELKE, M.A.,

OF LINCOLN'S INN, BARRISTER-AT-LAW.

LONDON:

STEVENS & HAYNES,

𝕷𝖆𝖜 𝖕𝖚𝖇𝖑𝖎𝖘𝖍𝖊𝖗𝖘,

BELL YARD, TEMPLE BAR.

1880.

LONDON
BRADBURY, AGNEW, & CO., PRINTERS, WHITEFRIARS.

PREFACE.

—•—

THE *raison d'être* of this little book is twofold—(1) it
aims at recording all the important practice cases in the
Chancery and three Common Law Divisions decided with
reference to the Judicature Acts down to the present
moment in the briefest possible language, (2) of doing so
in immediate connection with the wording of the Acts and
Rules themselves. It is in no sense a "setting out" of
the Acts and Rules, of which many portions have been
omitted, some as purely transitional and now already of
little more than antiquarian interest, some as simply
directing official routine, others as not having given occasion for any judicial interpretation, and as perhaps not
being likely to do so. After one half-decade of experience
of the working of the Acts, it has seemed to the writer
that the time had arrived for an endeavour to consolidate
the gist of the decisions along with the portions they in-
terpret, adding further an epitome of just so much of
other parts of the Acts and Rules as would form a connected whole. In condensing the combination, it is not

anticipated that any real difficulty can arise from the frequent use of such abbreviations as e.g. "generally "= " unless the Court or a Judge shall otherwise order," or " on terms "=" on such terms as to costs or otherwise as to the Court or a Judge shall seem fit," &c. ; especially as it is assumed that the reader possesses some edition of the Acts and Rules.

The various subjects interlace at so many points, that it is perhaps impossible to frame a perfectly scientific division ; but it will be seen that the main lines of an action have been followed, various miscellaneous points being left to the concluding part. One innovation will be noticed, in that counter-claim is made to follow directly after claim, most of the regulations as to the one obviously applying, *mutatis mutandis*, to the other. The writer is not so sanguine as to suppose that he has been always successful in his attempt at condensation and abbreviation. Where he has failed, he trusts that the notes will at least serve as an index for the correction of his errors. Where and so far as he may have succeeded in presenting a brief *primâ facie* view of the joint product of statute and "judge-made" Law as at this moment existing, he is well aware that in this, perhaps even more than in any other branch of Law, the infinite possibilities of variation and combination, together with that large discretion which the elasticity of the Acts and Rules allows to the Court, must prevent any chance of a finality where all points shall be " concluded by authority."

The writer desires to acknowledge his obligations, as to the earlier cases, to the various editions of the Acts, particularly those of Mr. Wilson and Sir W. T. Charley. It is hoped that the book will be found complete as regards cases reported in the Law Reports down to the present moment. And it has been attempted to combine with these all the more important cases given in the Weekly Notes, and in various other Reports.

W. H. H. K.

77, CHANCERY LANE,
        November, 1880.

CONTENTS.

— ◆ —

TABLE OF CASES . . . . . .

PART I. PRELIMINARY. THE ACTS .

„ II. WRIT TO CLOSE OF PLEADINGS

„ III. EVIDENCE, &c. . . . .

„ IV. TRIAL TO EXECUTION . .

„ V. APPEAL—COSTS .

„ VI. MISCELLANEOUS . . .

—

INDEX

CONTENTS

TABLE OF CASES.

PAGE

A.

Abud v. Riches . . . 69
Adams, In re . . . 86
Alforth v. Espinach . . 28
"Alina" 10
Allen v. Kennet . . . 32
Allhusen v. Labouchere . 48, 49
Ambroise v. Evelyn . . 37, 45
Amics v. Clark . . . 8
Amos v. Chadwick . . . 90
Anderson v. Bank of British Columbia . . . 51
Anderson v. Titmas . . . 64
Anglo-Italian Bank v. Davies 6, 21, 70
Anstey v. North and South Woolwich Subway Co. . . . 49
Anthony v. Halstead . . 64
Appleford v. Judkins . . 3, 8
Arkwright v. Newbold . . 85
Ashley v. Taylor . . 27
Ashurst v. Outram . . . 77
Associated Home Co. v. Whichcord 30
Aston v. Hurwitz . . 13
Atherley v. Harvey . . 6, 49
Atkins' Estate, In re . . 28
Attenborough v. London and St. Katherine's Dock Co. . . 33
Attorney-General v. Birmingham (Council of) . . 26
——— v. Constable . 99
——— v. Metropolitan Railway Co. 55
——— v. Pagham Harbour Reclamation Co. . 56
——— v. Shrewsbury Bridge Co. . 12

Attorney-General v. Swansea Improvement & Tramway Co. 82
——— v. Tomline . 68
Atwood v. Chichester . . 45

B.

Back v. Hay . . . 59
Bacon v. Bacon . . . 51
Bagnall v. Carlton . . 72
Bagot v. Easton . . 4, 30, 31, 43
Baigent v. Baigent . . 69
Baillie's Trusts, In re . . 80
Baker v. Oakes . . . 96
Banco de Portugal, Ex parte . 2
——— v. Waddell . 75
Bank of Whitehaven v. Thompson . 15
Banque Franco - Egyptienne v. Lutscher . . . 55
Barber v. Mackrell . . 54
Barr v. Barr . . . 6
Bartholomew v. Freeman . 91
Barton v. Titchmarsh . . 3
Bates v. Eley . . . 56
Beaney v. Elliott . . 22
Beckingham v. Owen . . 21
Beddington v. Beddington . 14
Beddow v. Beddow . . 5
Begg v. Cooper . . . 20
Bell v. North Staffordshire Railway Co. . . . 94
——— v. Wilkinson . . . 41
Bellaby v. Grant . . 15
Belmonte v. Aynard . . 85
Benbow v. Low . . 35
Beneke v. Frost . . 29

	PAGE
Bennett r. Lord Bury	90
—— r. Moore	67
Berdan v. Birmingham Small Arms Co.	79
—— r. Greenwood	43
Berkeley r. Standard Discount Co.	48
Berridge r. Roberts	21
Berry r. Exchange Trading Co.	93
Beynon r. Godden	83
Bidder r. North Staffordshire Railway Co.	3
Bigsby r. Dickinson	56, 75, 77
Birmingham Estates Co. r. Smith	33, 34, 35
—— Waste Co. r. Lane	98
Blackburn Union r. Brooks	55
Blake v. Albion Life Assurance Co.	43
—— r. Appleyard	35
—— r. Beech	3
Blewitt v. Dowling	4
Blyth and Young, In re	80
Boddy r. Wall	42
Bolivia (Republic of) r. National Bolivian Navigation Co.	66
Bolton v. Bolton	55
Booth r. Briscoe	22
Bordier r. Burrell	58
Bower r. Hartley	29
Bowey r. Bell	83
Boyes r. Cook	37
Boyle v. Bettwys Llantwit Collieries Co.	6
Poynton r. Boynton	28
Braginton r. Yates	9, 62
Bramble, Ex parte	91
Breton r. Crockett	37
Brewster r. Durrand	66
Bridson r. Smith	67
Bright c. Campbell	28
British Dynamite Co. r. Krebs	93
—— Imperial Co., In re	16
Brocklebank r. King's Lynn Steam Ship Co.	84
Brooke r. Wigg	51
Brown r. Trotman	72
Browning r. Sabin	68
Bryant, In re	68
—— r. Bull	6
Buckton r. Higgs	39
Budding c. Murdoch	42
Buenos Ayres and Ensenada Port Railway Co r. Northern Railway Co. of Buenos Ayres	16
Bullock r. Corry	51

	PAGE
Burgoine r. Taylor	61
Burke r. Rooney	44
Burns r. Irving	72
Burnell r. Burnell	7, 67
Bustros r. Bustros	17
—— r. White	50, 51
Butler r. Butler	30
Byrd r. Nunn	36

C.

	PAGE
CALDWELL r. Pagham Harbour Reclamation Co.	43
Caley r. Caley	24
Callander r. Hawkins	38
Campbell r. Fairlie	8
—— r. Holyland	93
Capes r. Brewer	14
Cargill r. Bower	42
"Cartburn"	30
Cartwright, Mary, In the goods of,	69, 93
Casey r. Arnott	16
Cashin r. Cradock	43, 50, 52
Catling r. King	41
Central African Trading Co. r. Grove	30
Chamberlain r. Barnwell	77
Champion r. Formby	38
Chapman r. Knight	7
—— r. Mason	90
—— r. Midland Railway Co.	86
—— r. Real Property Trust	89
Chatfield r. Sedgwick	35
Chester r. Phillips	25
Chesterfield, &c., Colliery Co. v. Black	49
Child r. Stenning	22, 23, 31
Chilton r. Corporation of London	66
Chorlton r. Dickie	29, 60
Church r. Perry	49
Clark r. Callow	36
Clarke r. Cookson	59
—— r. Roche	3, 81
Clutton r. Lee	93
Cobbold c. Pyke	10
Cockle r. Joyce	61
Cockshott r. London General Cab Co.	60
Cole r. Firth	33
Colebourne r. Colebourne	5, 12
Collette r. Goode	36
Collins r. Vestry of Paddington,	74, 79, 80
—— r. Welch	83
Commissioners of Sewers, &c. r. Gellatly	25

	PAGE
Conington v. Gilliatt	60
Conybeare v. Lewis	45
Cook v. Dey	14, 33
—— v. Enchmarch	32
Cooper v. Blisset	25
—— v. Whittingham	5
Costa Rica (Republic of) v. Erlanger	48, 84
—— —— v. Strousberg	50
Cousins v. Lombard Deposit Bank	7
Cowan's Estate, In re	70, 71
Cox v. Barker	23, 31
Cracknall v. Janson	49, 76, 86
Craig v. Phillips	79
Crane v. Jullion	14
Credit Foncier of Mauritius v. Paturau	3
Creen v. Wright	83
Cremetti v. Crom	70, 71
Creswell v. Parker	16, 17
Crom v. Samuels	94
Crowe v. Barnicot	35
Crowle v. Russell	4
Crump v. Cavendish	20
Crush v. Turner	7
Cummins v. Herron	78

D.

Dallinger v. St. Albyn	42
Darcy v. Whittaker	27
Daubney v. Shuttleworth	93
Daun v. Simmins	68
Davies v. Felix	63
—— v. Garland	14
—— v. Williams	52
Davis v. Flagstaff Mining Co. of Utah	35
—— v. Goodbehere	63
—— v. Spence	20
Davy v. Garrett	33, 43
Dawkins v. Lord Penrhyn	41
—— v. Prince Edward of Saxe-Weimar	4
Dawson v. Shepherd	31
Day v. Whittaker	88
Dean v. Wilson	5, 7, 92, 97
Dear v. Sworder	30
De Hart v. Stevenson	27
Delmar v. Freemantle	12, 92
Dence v. Mason	81
Dennis v. Seymour	21

	PAGE
Dessilla v. Schunck & Co. and Fels & Co.	31
Diamond Fuel Co., In re	80
Dicks v. Brooks	75
Dickson v. Harrison	79
Disney v. Longbourne	47
Ditton, Ex parte	87
Dix v. Groom	80
Dodds v. Shepherd	9, 32
Dollman v. Jones	63
Donovan v. Brown	82
Dowdeswell v. Dowdeswell	5, 23
Doyle v. Kaufman	96
Duchess of Westminster Silver Lead Ore Co., In re	76
Duckett v. Gover	41
Duckitt v. Jones	37
Dunkirk Colliery Co. v. Lever	62
Dupuy v. Welsford	24
Durling v. Lawrence	42
Dymond v. Croft	15, 18, 33, 70
Dyson v. Pickles	98

E.

Eade v. Jacobs	49
Eden v. Naish	4
Edmunds v. Attorney-General	4
Edwards v. Edwards	6, 68
Egremont Burial Board v. Egremont Iron Ore Co.	50
Elam v. Vaughan	26
Eldridge v. Burgess	27, 61
"Elijah Packer"	84
Ellis v. Ambler	47
—— v. Munson	34
Emma Silver Mining Co. v. Grant	60, 82
English v. Tuttie	51
Etty v. Wilson	63
Evans, Ex parte	6
—— v. Buck	22
—— v. Puleston	92
Evelyn v. Evelyn	33
—— v. Hughes	3

F.

Faithfull v. Ewen	71
Fardon's Vinegar Co., Ex parte	77
Faund v. Wallace	64
Field v. Field	90
— v. Great Northern Railway Co.	83

PAGE

Finlay v. Davis 39
Kinney v. Hinde . . . 29, 72
Fisher v. Owen 49
Fleming v. Manchester & Sheffield
   Railway Co.. 9
Flower v. Lloyd . . . 75, 81
Forrest v. Davis 94
Fortescue v. Fortescue . . 52
Foster v. Gamgee . . . 38
—— v. Roberts . . . 65
Fox v. Wallis . . . 94
Fraser v. Burrows . . . 4, 52
Freason v. Loe . . . 60
Freeman v. Cox . . . 54, 92
Friend v. London, Chatham, &
   Dover Railway Co. . . . 51
Fritz v. Hobson 67
Fryer v. Royle . . . 25
Furness v. Booth . . 30

G.

GALATTI v. Wakefield . . 84
Garbett v. Fawcus . . 4
Gardner, In re 92
—— v. Irvin . . 52
Garnet v. Bradley . . . 83
Gaskin v. Balls . . . 6
Gathercole v. Smith . . 74
Gatti v. Webster . . 22
Gay v. Labouchere . . . 49
Gibbons v. London Financial Asso-
   ciation 94
Gilbert v. Endean . . 56
—— v. Smith . . . 66, 67
Gillott v. Kerr . . . 44, 67
"Glannibanta" . . . 76
Gledhill v. Hunter . . . 32
Golding v. Wharton Saltworks Co. 43
Graham v. Campbell . . . 76
Grane v. Taylor . . . 92
Grant v. Banque Franco-Egyptienne 80, 81
—— v. Holland 6
Great Australian Gold Mining Co.
   v. Martin 16
Greaves v. Fleming . . . 39
Green v. Coleby . . . 37
—— v. Pratt . . 24
—— v. Sevin . . . 35
Griffin, Ex parte . . . 86
—— v. Allen . . . 78
Grills v. Dillon . . 81

PAGE

H.

H. v. H. 5
Hagg v. Darley 41
Hall v. Eve 40
Hamer v. Giles . . . 71
Hamilton v. Davies . . . 15
Hamilton & Co. v. Johnson & Co. 66
Hancock v. Guerin . . . 47
—— v. Lablache . . . 24
Hankins v. Turner . . . 81
Hanmer v. Flight 67
Harbord v. Monk . . . 47
Harris v. Aaron 76
—— v. Fleming . . . 16
—— v. Gamble . . . 35, 58
—— v. Owners of "Franconia" 16
—— v. Petherick . . . 83
—— v. Warre . . . 36
Harrison v. Bottenheim . . 21
—— v. Wearing . . . 87
Harry v. Davey . . . 29
Hartley v. Dilke . . . 14
—— v. Owen 53
Hasker, In re 78
Hastie v. Hastie . . . 74, 75
Hate v. Snelling . . . 45
Hawksley v. Bradshaw . . 39, 43
Hawley v. Reade . . . 47
Heap v. Marris . . . 43
Hedley v. Bates . . . 4, 6
Hennessy v. Bohmann, &c., & Co. 5, 49
Hetherington v. Longrigg . . 67
Hough v. Chamberlain . . 43
Higginbotham v. Aynsley . 37, 44
Higginson v. Hall . . . 50
Higgs v. Schrader . . . 72
Highton v. Treherne . . 79
Hillman v. Mayhew . . 11, 40, 89
Hill's Executors v. Managers of
   Metropolitan Asylum District. 77
Hobbs v. Reid . . . 25
Hoch v. Boor . . . 9, 62
Hodges v. Fincham . . . 70
—— v. Hodges . . . 37
Hodgson v. Fox . . . 11
Hodson v. Mochi . . . 35
Holloway v. York . . . 33
Holmes v. Hervey . . . 59
Holt v. Jesse . . . 8
Homer v. Oyler . . . 86
Honduras Inter-Oceanic Railway
   Co. v. Tucker . . . 23
Hooke v. Ind, Coope, & Co. . 33

	PAGE
Hoole v. Earnshaw	39
Hopewell v. Barnes	72
Horwell v. London General Omnibus Co.	29
Hoskins' Trusts, In re	76
Houseman v. Houseman	4, 7
Huckwell, In re	37
Huggons v. Tweed	34
Hughes v. Metropolitan Railway Co.	4
Humphreys v. Edwards	11, 89
Hunt v. City of London Real Property Co.	60, 62
Hunter v. Hunter	75
—— v. Young	30
Hutchins v. Glover	51
Hyde v. Warden	91

I.

	PAGE
International Financial Society v. City of Moscow Gas Co.	79
Ireland, Ex parte	79
Irlam v. Irlam	54, 93, 97
Isaacs, Ex parte	81
Ivory, In re	81

J.

	PAGE
Jackson v. North Eastern Railway Co.	28
James v. Crow	61
Jenkins v. Davies	67
—— v. Morris	62, 64
Job v. Job	11
Johnasson v. Bonhote	41
Johns v. James	49
Johnson v. Smith	51
Jones, In re	14
—— v. Baxter	62, 63
—— v. Chennel	76
—— v. Jones	9
—— v. Monte Video Gas Co.	52
Joselyne, Ex parte	71
Judd v. Green	81
"Julia Fisher"	85
Jupp v. Cooper	68
Justice v. Mersey Steel and Iron Co.	82

K.

	PAGE
Kain v. Farrer	51

	PAGE
Keate v. Phillips	27
Kendall v. Hamilton	25
Kelly v. Byles	76
King v. Corke	43
—— v. Davenport	44, 96
—— v. Sandeman	61
Kingchurch v. People's Garden Co.	4
Kino v. Rudkin	26
Kirkwood v. Webster	77
Knatchbull v. Fowler	54
Knight v. Pursell	87
Krehl v. Burrell	63

L.

	PAGE
La Grange v. McAndrew	44
"Lake Megantic"	80
Laming v. Gee	11
Landore Siemen Steel Co., In re	90
Langley, In re	68
Langridge v. Campbell	39
Lascelles v. Butt	57, 62
"Laurella"	76
Lawrence, In re	78
Lawrenson v. Dublin Metropolitan Junction Railway Co.	15
Le Blanch v. Reuter's Telegraph Co.	8
Lee v. Nuttall	11, 81
Lee Conservancy Board v. Button	77
Lees v. Patterson	35
Lewis v. Nobbs	24
Liberia (Republic of) v. Roye	50
Little's Case	74
Litton v. Litton	40, 67
Lloyd, In re	6
—— v. Dimmack	23, 29
—— v. Jones	59, 90
—— v. Lewis	65
Lloyd, Allen & Lloyd, In re	6
Lloyd's Banking Co. v. Ogle	20
London v. Roffey	63
London Joint Stock Bank v. Aldermen of London	72
London Joint Stock Bank v. Mayor of London	72
London and Provincial Maritime Insurance Co. v. Davies	47
London Syndicate v. Lord	54, 91
Longbottom, Ex parte	8
Longman v. East	9, 62
Lowe v. Lowe	63
Lows, Ex parte	61

PAGE

Luckie, *In re* 16
Luke *v.* South Kensington Hotel
　Co. 25
Lumb *v.* Whiteley . . . 98
Lydall *v.* Martinson . . . 61
Lyon *v.* Tweddell . . . 49

M.

McAllister *v.* Bishop of Rochester 31, 50
McAndrew *v.* Barker 9, 33, 63, 79, 80
McCorquodale *v.* Bell . . 50, 51
MacDonald *v.* Carrington . . 32
—— *v.* Foster . . 7, 97
McPhail *v.* Lowder . . . 17
Machu *v.* O'Connor . . . 77
Mackley *v.* Chillingworth . . 86
Manchester and Milford Railway
　Co., *In re* 6
Manchester, Sheffield, and Lincoln
　Railway Co. *v.* Brooks . . 22
Mansfield *v.* Childerhouse . . 49
Maples *v.* Masini . . . 33
Marner *v.* Bright . . 4, 30
Marriott *v.* Marriott . . 42
Marsden *v.* Lancashire and York-
　shire Railway Co. . . 83
Martano *v.* Mann . . . 23
Martin *v.* Bannister . . . 10
—— *v.* Gale . . . 67
Mason *v.* Brentini . . . 34
—— *v.* Wirral Highway Board . 72
Massey *v.* Allen . . . 84
Masters, *Ex parte* . . . 77
Matthews *v.* Whittle . . 32
May *v.* Head . . . 61
Mayer *v.* Murray . . . 11
Mellor *v.* Denham . . . 3
—— *v.* Sidebotham . . 67
Mercantile Mutual Insurance Co. *v.*
　Shoesmith . . . 47
Mercer's Co., *Ex parte* . . 83
Mercier *v.* Cotton . . . 47
Metropolitan Asylum District *v.*
　Hill 8
Metropolitan Bank *v.* Heiron . 63
Metropolitan Board of Works *v.*
　New River Co. . . . 95
Metropolitan Inner Circle Railway
　Co. *v.* Metropolitan Railway
　Co. 58
Metropolitan Railway Co. *v.* De-
　fries 12

PAGE

Meyrick *v.* James . . . 56
Michell *v.* Wilson . . . 61
Michell's Trusts, *In re* . . 79
Middleton *v.* Pollock . . 27
Millard *v.* Burroughes . . 88
Mills *v.* Jennings . . . 23
Millissich *v.* Lloyd's . . 66
Minton *v.* Metcalf . . . 33
Molloy *v.* Kilby . . . 48
Morgan *v.* Elford . . . 82
Morton *v.* Miller . . . 32
Mostyn *v.* West Mostyn Coal and
　Iron Co. 3, 7
Muirhead *v.* Direct United States
　Cable Co. . . . 20
Mullins *v.* Howell . . . 93
Murr *v.* Cooke . . . 9
Mycock *v.* Beatson . . . 31
Myers *v.* Defries . . . 83

N.

Nagle-Gillman *v.* Christopher . 57
Nathan *v.* Batchelor . . . 40
National Funds Assurance Co.,
　In re 78, 80
Naylor *v.* Farrer . . . 34
Neale *v.* Clarke . . 9, 33
Nelson, *Ex parte* . . . 73
New British Mutual Investment Co.
　v. Peed . . . 51
New River Co. *v.* Midland Railway
　Co. 80
New Westminster Brewery Co. *v.*
　Hannah 54
Newbiggin-by-the-Sea Gas Co. *v.*
　Armstrong . . 11, 14
Newcomen *v.* Coulson . . 46
Newell *v.* Provincial Bank of Eng-
　land . . . 3, 35
Noad *v.* Murrow . . . 36
Nobel's Explosive Co. *v.* Jones, &c. 42
Noel *v.* Noel . . 23, 24
Norris *v.* Beazley . . . 27
Northampton Coal and Iron Co. *v.*
　Midland Waggon Co. . 42, 84, 85
Northumberland (Duke of) *v.* Todd 56
Norton *v.* Florence Land, &c., Co. 16
—— *v.* London & North-Western
　Railway Co. . . . 79
Noyes *v.* Crawley . . . 41
Nurse *v.* Durnford . . . 14

PAGE

O.

Oakwell Collieries, In re . 92
Oastler v. Henderson . . . 63
O'Neile v. Clason . . . 14
Oriental Bank v. Fitzgerald . . 20
Original Hartlepool Collieries v.
 Gibb 34, 38
Orr-Ewing & Co. v. Johnson &
 Co. 77
Orr-Ewing's Trademarks, In re . 83
Ortner v. Fitzgibbon . . . 20
Owen v. Henshaw . . . 72, 97
—— v. Wynn 50

P.

Padley v. Camphausen . . . 15
Padwick v. Scott 34
Pannell v. Nunn 64
Papayanni v. Coutpas . . . 21
Paraire v. Loibl 39
Paris Skating Rink Co., In re . 29
Parker, In re 28
Parpaite Frères v. Dickenson . 13
Parsons v. Harris . . . 45, 66
—— v. Tinling 83
Payne, Ex parte 76
Peacock v. Hooper . . . 56
Pearse v. Spickett . . . 45
Pease v. Fletcher 5
Peck v. Trinsmaran Iron Co. . . 6
Pellas v. Neptune . . . 34
People's Garden Co., In re . . 4
Percy and Kelly Nickel, &c., Co.,
 In re 85
Perkins v. Dangerfield . . . 68
Peru (Republic of) v. Weguelin . 82
Pheysey v. Pheysey . . . 80
Philipps v. Philipps . . . 87
Phillips & Gill, In re . . 12, 93
—— v. Phillips . . . 43
—— v. South-Western Railway
 Co. 64
Phosphate Sewage Co. v. Hartmont 80
—— v. Molleson . . . 4
Pierpoint v. Cartwright . . 7
Pike v. Keene . . . 25, 53
Pilcher, In re 96
—— v. Hinds 32
Pilley v. Baylis 59
Polini v. Gray . . . 81, 82
Pontifex v. Midland Railway Co. . 9

PAGE

Pontifex v. Severn . . . 9, 62
Pooley v. Bosanquet . . . 93
—— v. Driver . . . 86, 95
Potter v. Chambers . . 9, 35
—— v. Cotton 64
Powell v. Jewsbury . . . 41
—— v. Williams . . 58, 59
Pringle v. Gloag . . . 86, 87
Protector Endowment Co. v. Whit-
 ham 71
Pullen v. Snelus 36
Purnell v. Great Western Railway
 Co. and Harris . . 64, 74, 96

R.

Rafael v. Ongley . . . 14
Ralph v. Carrick . . . 76
Ray v. Barker . . . 20, 21
Real and Personal Advance Co. v.
 McCarthy . . . 6, 46
Reddish, Ex parte . . . 75
Redmayne v. Vaughan . . . 58
Redondo v. Chaytor . . . 85
Rees, In re 26
Regina v. Fletcher . . . 3
—— v. Pemberton . . . 8
—— v. Steel 3
—— v. Swindon New Town Local
 Board 7
Renshaw v. Renshaw . . . 33
Rhodes v. Airedale Draining Com-
 missioners . . . 3
—— v. Jenkins . . . 79
Richards v. Kitchen . . . 68
Richardson, In re . . . 87
Richardson v. Elmit . . . 70
Robarts v. Buée . . . 86
Roberts v. Evans . . 23, 24
Robertson v. Howard . . . 40
Robinson v. Chadwick . . . 90
Roe v. Davies . . . 43, 56
Rogers v. Jones . . . 85
—— v. Manby . . . 56
Rolfe v. Maclaren . . 35, 54, 67
Ross v. Gibbs 51
Rotheram v. Priest . . . 20
Roupell v. Parsons . . . 45
Rowcliffe v. Leigh . . 48, 49, 50
Royle, In re 12
Rumsey v. Reade . . 54, 67
Runnacles v. Mesquita . . 20
Runtz v. Sheffield . . . 94

	PAGE
Ruston r. Tobin	27, 59
Rutter c. Tregent	67

S.

Saffery, Ex parte	79, 95
St. Nazaire Co., In re	2, 42, 75
Sanderson, In re	86
Saner r. Bilton	34
Saunders r. Jones	49
Sargant r. Read	91
Sawyer, Ex parte	77
Saxby c. Easterbank	5
—— r. Gloucester Waggon Co.	9
Scott r. Royal Wax Candle Co.	15
Schröder r. Central Bank of London	5
Scutt r. Freeman	61, 65
Seymour r. Coulson	7
Sharrock r. London & North Western Railway Co.	7, 78
Shaw r. Earl of Jersey	6
Shelford r. Louth & East Coast Railway Co.	20
Sheward c. Lord Lonsdale	49
Shippey c. Grey	71
Shoetensack c. Price & Co.	78
Siddons r. Lawrence	83
Simmons r. Storer	87
Singer Manufacturing Co. v. Lovg	59
Slade v. Tucker	51
Sloman r. Governor of New Zealand	15
Smith, Ex parte	29
—— In re	97
—— r. Berg	49
—— r. Dobbin	13, 17, 19
—— r. Grindley	78
—— r. Richardson	22, 31
—— r. Wilson	13
Smyth, In re	53
Snell, In re	87
Solicitor, In re a	68
Southwark and Vauxhall Waterworks Co. v. Quick	50
Spiller v. Paris Skating Rink Co.	55
Spratt's Patent v. Ward & Co.	59
Sprunt v. Pugh	73
Spurr r. Hall	43
Stahlschmidt r. Walford	46
Standard Discount Co. c. La Grange	80
Staples r. Young	35
Steel c. Dixon	30

	PAGE
Stewart r. Gladstone	54
Stirling r. Du Barry	94
Stockton Iron Furnace Co., In re	75
Stokes r. Grant	43
Stone c. Bennet	28
Storey r. Waddle	89
Street r. Gover	38
Stubbs' Estate, In re	90
—— r. Boyle	62, 66
Sugden r. Lord St. Leonards	76
Sugg r. Silber	58
Sutcliffe r. James	36
Swansea (Mayor of) r. Quirk	48
Swansea Shipping Co. r. Duncan	16, 17, 29, 31
Swindell r. Birmingham Syndicate	59, 78
Sykes r. Firth	59
Symonds v. Jenkins	67

T.

Tasmanian Main Line Railway Co. r. Clark	60
Tawell r. Slate Co.	32
Taylor's Case	79
Taylor r. Batten	52
—— r. Eckersley	6
—— r. Keily	52
—— c. Jones	94
Tennant r. Rawlings	82
Thomas c. Elsom	74
—— r. Williams	5, 59
Thompson r. Marshall	21
—— r. Woodfine	34
Thorley Cattle Food Co. v. Massam	5
Thorn r. Smith	15
Thorp r. Holdsworth	36, 67
Tildesley r. Harper	36, 43, 67
Tilney r. Stansfield	69
Timms, In re	90
Tomline r. Queen	52
Tottenham r. Barry	16, 17
Traill r. Jackson	79
Treleven r. Bray	29
Trotter's Claim	74
Trowell r. Shenton	41, 80
Turner c. Hednesford Gas Co.	4, 30
—— r. Heyland	83
—— c. Samson	41
Turquand v. Wilson	54, 67
Twycross v. Dreyfus	16
—— v. Grant	27

U.

Union Bank of London v. Manby . . 47, 50, 52
Usil v. Brearley 80

V.

Val de Travers Asphalte Co. v. London Tramways Co. . . 26
Vale v. Oppert 81
Vallance v. Birmingham & Midland Land Investment Corporation 26
Vavasseur v. Krupp . . 34, 45
"Victoria" 80
Viney, Ex parte 79

W.

Waddell v. Blockey . . 66, 81
Walker v. Budden . . . 82
—— v. Hicks 13
Wallis v. Hepburn . . . 44
—— v. Lichfield . . . 61
Wallingford v. Mutual Society . 21
Walsall Overseers v. London and North Western Railway Co. . 3
Ward, Ex parte . . 75, 80
—— v. Hall . . . 9
—— v. Pilley . . . 9, 60
—— v. Wyld . . 84, 98
Warner v. Murdoch . . . 59
Warraker v. Pryer . . . 25
Watson v. Rodwell . . 43, 54
Watt v. Barnett . . . 14
Webb v. East . . . 53
—— v. Mansell . . . 77
Webster v. Whewall . . 53
Wedderburn v. Pickering . . 59
Wells v. Mitcham Gas Co. . . 77
Welsh Steam Coal Collieries Co. v. Gaskell 52
West v. White . . 58, 59
West of England Bank v. Canton Insurance Co. . . . 50
West of England Bank v. Nickolls 49

Westbourne Grove Drapery Stores, In re 10
Western of Canada Oil Co., In re . 55
Westman v. Aktiebolaget, &c. . . 15
Whetstone v. Dewis . . . 32
Whistler v. Hancock . . . 44
Whitaker v. Thurston . . . 33
White v. Bromige . . . 42
—— v. Witt . . 76, 78
Whittle, Ex parte . . . 79
Whitley v. Honeywell . . . 14
Whittaker v. Robinson . . . 90
Widgeon v. Tepper . . . 72
Wilk's Trustees, &c., v. Judge . 80
Wilkins v. Bedford . . . 61
Willcock v. Terrell . . . 73
Williams v. Bindon . . . 8
—— v. Bolland . . . 10
—— v. Richardson . . . 32
—— v. Snowdon . . . 4
Williamson v. London and North-Western Railway Co. . 39, 40, 43
Wilson v. Church 26, 27, 48, 67, 81, 82
—— v. Smith . . 80, 81
Wingrove v. Thompson . . 28
Winterfield v. Bradnum . . 63
Witham v. Vane . . . 31
Witt v. Corcoran . . . 8
—— v. Parker . . . 9
Wood and Ivery v. Hamblet . . 60
Wood v. Kay . . . 59
Woods v. McInnes . . . 17
Woolf v. Pemberton . . . 24
Wortley, In re . . . 90
Wright v. Clifford . . . 61
—— v. Redgrave . . . 4
—— v. Swindon Railway Co. 28, 44
Wymer v. Dodds . . . 26

Y.

Yetts v. Foster . . . 63
Yorkshire Banking Co. v. Beatson 21
Yorkshire Waggon Co. v. Newport Coal Co. . . . 31
Young v. Brassey . . 16, 17
—— v. Kitchen . . . 5, 34

A DIGEST

OF THE

LAW OF PRACTICE.

PART I.

PRELIMINARY.—THE ACTS.

1. THE Supreme Court of Judicature consists of two permanent Divisions, of which

A. The High Court of Justice exercises original jurisdiction with certain appellate jurisdiction from Inferior Courts ;

B. The Court of Appeal exercises appellate jurisdiction with such original jurisdiction as is incident thereto, including all the powers and duties as to amendment and otherwise of a Court of First Instance (*a*).

A. The High Court of Justice is a Superior Court of Record, and has vested in it the jurisdiction formerly vested in (1) the High Court of Chancery, (2) the Court of Queen's Bench, (3) the Court of Common Pleas, (4) the Court of Exchequer as a Court of Revenue, as well as a Common Law Court, (5) the High Court of Admiralty, (6) the Court of Probate, (7) the Court for Divorce and Matrimonial Causes, (8) the Court of Common Pleas at Lancaster, (9) the Court of Pleas at Durham, (10) the Courts created by commission of Assize, of Oyer and Terminer, and of Gaol Delivery, or any of such commissions (*b*) ; but not

(*a*) Judicature Act, 1873, s. 4, and O. LVIII. r. 5.
(*b*) S. 16.

B

(1) Any appellate jurisdiction of the Court of Appeal in Chancery or of the same Court sitting as a Court of Appeal in Bankruptcy [and no Judge of the High Court has jurisdiction to rehear an Order made by him or another judge (c)], nor (2) any jurisdiction of the Court of Appeal in Chancery of the County Palatine of Lancaster, nor (3) any jurisdiction vested in the Lord Chancellor in relation to lunacy, &c., grants of Letters Patent, Commissions, &c., under the Great Seal, jurisdiction of the Lord Chancellor on behalf of Her Majesty as Visitor of any College or Charitable or other foundation, nor (4) any jurisdiction of the Master of the Rolls in relation to records (d).

B. The Court of Appeal is a Superior Court of Record, and has vested in it the jurisdiction and powers of (1) the Lord Chancellor and the Court of Appeal in Chancery and the same Court as a Court of Appeal in Bankruptcy [but whether including jurisdiction to rehear an appeal under the Bankruptcy Act, 1869, quære (e)], (2) the Court of Appeal in Chancery of the County Palatine of Lancaster, (3) the Court of the Lord Warden of the Stannaries, (4) the Court of Exchequer Chamber (f).

2. Subject to the consent of the Attorney-General, where necessary (g), and to conditions imposed by Order of the House of Lords as to value of subject-matter, security for costs, time within which appeal may be brought, and generally all matters of practice and procedure (h), and omitting cases where appeal did not formerly lie to the House of Lords and shall not hereafter be authorised by Orders of the said House (i), an appeal lies to the House of Lords from any Order or Judgment of (1) the Court of Appeal in England; (2) any Court in Scotland from which error or appeal previously lay to the House of Lords by Common Law or Statute ; (3) any Court in Ireland from which error or appeal similarly lay (j).

(c) *In re St. Nazaire Co.*, 12 Ch. D. 88.
(d) S. 17.
(e) *Ex parte Banco de Portugal, re Hooper*, 14 Ch. D. 1.
(f) S. 18.
(g) App. Jurisd. Act, 1876, s. 10.
(h) Do. s. 11.
(i) Do. s. 12.   (j) Do. s. 3.

3. An appeal lies in Ecclesiastical Cases, and from Indian and all Colonial Courts, Channel Islands, and Isle of Man, to the Judicial Committee of the Privy Council (*k*). But no such appeal can be brought as to costs alone (*l*).

4. The Court of Appeal has jurisdiction to hear appeals from any Judgment or Order of the High Court of Justice, or of any judge or judges thereof (*m*), including a judgment of the Queen's Bench on a case stated by a Court of Quarter Sessions (*n*), and a decision of the High Court on a special case stated by an umpire under the Lands Clauses Consolidation Act, 1845 (*o*), but not including appeals in the first instance from Inferior Courts, which should be made to a Divisional Court (*p*), whose determination shall be final, unless special leave to appeal to the Court of Appeal be given by such Divisional Court (*q*).

5. In every civil cause or matter commenced in the High Court of Justice law and equity shall be administered by the High Court of Justice and the Court of Appeal respectively, according to the rules following :—The said Courts respectively, and every judge thereof, shall give such effect as the Court of Chancery would have formerly given to every equitable estate, right, or ground of relief, alleged by any plaintiff (*r*) or defendant (*s*) ; and shall have power to grant to any defendant in respect of legal or equitable rights all relief properly claimed by his pleading against the plaintiff or against any other person duly served with notice in writing and thereby deemed a

(*k*) App. Jurisd. Act, 1876, s. 14.

(*l*) *Credit Foncier of Mauritius* v. *Paturau*, 35 L. T. 869.

(*m*) J. A. 1873, s. 19.

(*n*) *Walsall Overseers* v. *London and North Western Railway Co.*, 4 App. 30.

(*o*) *Bidder* v. *North Staffordshire Railway Co.*, 4 Q. B. D. 412, following *Rhodes* v. *Airedale Draining Commissioners*, 1 C. P. D. 402.

(*p*) *Clarke* v. *Roche*, 36 L. T. 727.

(*q*) S. 45, and see *Appleford* v. *Judkins*, 3 C. P. D. 489 ; *Barton* v. *Titchmarsh*, 49 L. J. Ch. D. 573 ; and on extent of jurisdiction of Court of Appeal in appeals on criminal cases see s. 47, *Reg* v. *Steel*, 2 Q. B. D. 37 ; *Reg.* v. *Fletcher*, 2 Q. B. D. 43 ; *Blake* v. *Beech*, 2 Ex. D. 335 ; *Mellor* v. *Denham*, 5 Q. B. D. 467.

(*r*) S. 24, sub-sec. (1).

(*s*) Do. (2). See *Mostyn* v. *West Mostyn Coal & Iron Co*, 1 C. P. D. 145 ; *Newell* v. *Provincial Bank of England*, 1 C. P. D. 496 ; *Eyre* v. *Hughes*, 2 Ch. D. 148.

party, provided such relief is connected with the original
subject of the cause or matter (*t*); and shall take notice
of equitable rights and duties appearing incidentally in
the course of any cause or matter (*u*). With or without
application by motion in a summary way on the part of
any person, whether a party or not, who would have been
formerly so entitled, either of the said Courts, if it shall
think fit, may direct a general or partial stay of proceedings in any cause or matter pending before it, and may
make such Order as shall be just (*v*).   Thus, *e.g.*, an
Order may be made where after decree the plaintiff is
found to have no title, and the applicant has been served
with notice of decree (*w*).   But an Order restraining an
action in another Division is bad where the party who
obtains it could not have done so formerly by injunction
in equity, and where the parties are not the same in the
two actions (*x*).   And the Chancery Division cannot
issue an injunction restraining a sheriff from selling
goods under a writ of another Division (*y*).   All such
remedies shall be granted as any parties appear to be
entitled to in respect of legal or equitable claims properly
brought forward, to the end that matters in controversy
may be finally determined (*z*).   And this end may be
reached by directing a stay of proceedings (*a*), which in
some cases may be done on application by summons (*b*).
But all necessary parties must be joined, as *e.g.* in an

(*t*) S. 24, sub-sec. (3). For rules as to counter-claim, see paragraphs
26, 27, 28; and as to third parties, pp. 21, 22, 23. See also *Turner* v.
Hednesford Gas Co., 3 Ex. D. 145; *Bagot* v. *Easton*, 11 Ch. D. 392;
Marner v. *Bright*, do. note.
(*u*) S. 24, sub-sec. (4). See *Hughes* v. *Metropolitan Railway Co.*, 1
C. P. D. 120, 2 App. Cas. 439; *Williams* v. *Snowdon*, W. N. 1880, 124.
(*v*) Do. (5).
(*w*) *Houseman* v. *Houseman*, 1 Ch. D. 535.
(*x*) *Crowle* v. *Russell*, 4 C. P. D. 186.
(*y*) *Wright* v. *Redgrave*, 11 Ch. D. 24. As to discretion of Court, see
Phosphate Sewage Co. v. *Molleson*, 1 App. C. 780; *Dawkins* v. *Prince
Edward of Saxe-Weimar*, 1 Q. B. D. 499; and generally *Garbutt* v. *Fawcus*,
1 Ch. D. 155; *Fraser* v. *Burrows*, 2 Q. B. D. 624; *Blewitt* v. *Dowling*,
W. N. 1875, 202. As to proceedings against a company pending a winding-
up petition, see *In re People's Garden Co.*, 1 Ch. D. 44; *Kingchurch* v.
People's Garden Co., 1 C. P. D. 45.
(*z*) S. 24 (7).
(*a*) *Eden* v. *Naish*, 7 Ch. D. 781; *Hedley* v. *Bates*, 13 Ch. D. 498.
(*b*) *Edmonds* v. *Attorney General*, 47 L. J. Ch. D. 345.

administration action the general administrator of an intestate (c).

6. All legal and other remedies for the recovery of a chose in action shall pass to the assignee by a proper assignment (d), but it does not follow *e converso* that a plaintiff can necessarily recover damages from the assignee for default of the assignor (e).

7. An injunction may be granted by an interlocutory Order, where it appears just or convenient, and whether the estates claimed are legal or equitable (f) or partly legal and partly equitable (g). The jurisdiction of the Court herein is practically unlimited. Thus, the assignment of a special penalty to a new statutory offence does not take away the remedy by injunction (h). And the Court can restrain an unfit or incompetent arbitrator (i) and the publication of a trade-libel, *semble*, even where not found such by a jury (j). But *semble*, it will not usually, on interlocutory motion, restrain an advertisement containing false representations (k), though it has power to do so, as where the matter has been found libellous by a jury (l), or where it concerns a sale ordered by the Court (m). Notice should be given of motion for an injunction (n).

8. Under similar circumstances a receiver may be appointed (o), but where such appointment is sought by action the writ of summons must be indorsed accordingly (p). But a receiver may be appointed even before service of writ in view of impending bankruptcy (q). Where the risk is immediate the plaintiff may be appointed interim receiver, even without security, as for fourteen

(c) *Dowdeswell* v. *Dowdeswell*, 9 Ch. D. 294.   (d) S. 25 (6).
(e) *Young* v. *Kitchen*, 3 Ex. D. 127 ; *Schröder* v. *Central Bank of London*, 34 L. T. 735.
(f) S. 25 (8).   (g) *Pease* v. *Fletcher*, 1 Ch. D. 273.
(h) *Cooper* v. *Whittingham*, 43 L. T. 16.
(i) *Beddow* v. *Beddow*, 9 Ch. D. 39.
(j) *Thomas* v. *Williams*, 43 L. T. 91 ; 14 Ch. D. 864.
(k) *Thorley Cattle Food Co.* v. *Massam*, 6 Ch. D. 582.
(l) *Saxby* v. *Easterbrook*, 3 C. P. D. 339.
(m) *Dean* v. *Wilson*, 10 Ch. D. 136.
(n) *Hennessy* v. *Bohman, Osborne and Co.*, W. N. 1877, 14.
(o) S. 25 (8).
(p) *Colebourne* v. *Colebourne*, 1 Ch. D. 690.
(q) *H.* v. *H.*, 1 Ch. D. 276.

days, or until one is appointed under reference to Chambers (r). But a party to an action should not generally be receiver without the assent of the other side (s). Yet an unpaid vendor has been appointed receiver to a Company without security or salary (t). One appointed " on giving security " is not receiver until it is given (u). An interim manager has been appointed in a foreclosure action brought by debenture-holders against a Company (v). The appointment of a receiver by a judgment creditor without any writ of *elegit* is a delivery in execution of equitable property (w). Where an action is pending in one Division application for a receiver should be made in that Division (x).

9. The granting of an injunction or appointment of a receiver may be unconditional or upon terms (y). Generally, it may be said that the old principle is enlarged but not altered (z).

10. Generally, the rules of Equity shall prevail (a). Hence, in Common Law Divisions, an order for changing a solicitor will be without provision for payment of his costs (b).

The causes and matters specially assigned to the Chancery Division comprise (*inter alia*)—(1) administration, (2) partnership and accounts, (3) redemption and foreclosure of mortgages, (4) portions, (5) sale of property subject to charges, (6) trusts, (7) rectification or cancellation of written instruments, (8) specific performance, (9) partition or sale, (10) care of infants and their estates (c).

(r) *Taylor* v. *Eckersley*, 2 Ch. D. 302.
(s) *In re Lloyd. Allen* v. *Lloyd*, 12 Ch. D. 447.
(t) *Boyle* v. *Bettoys Llantwit Colliery Co.*, 2 Ch. D. 276.
(u) *Edwards* v. *Edwards*, 2 Ch. D. 291.
(v) *Peek* v. *Trinsmaran Iron Co.*, 2 Ch. D. 115.
(w) *Ex parte Evans, Re Watkins*, 11 Ch. D. 769.
(x) *Barr* v. *Barr*, W. N. 1876, 44.
(y) S. 25 (8). For example of terms see *Shaw* v. *Earl of Jersey*, 4 C. P. D. 359.
(z) *Gaskin* v. *Ball*, 13 Ch. D. 324, 329. See also *Real and Personal Advance Co.* v. *M'Carthy*, 27 W. R. 706; *Anglo-Italian Bank* v. *Davies*, 9 Ch. D. 275; *Bryant* v. *Bull*, 10 Ch. D. 135; *Hedley* v. *Bates*, 13 Ch. D. 498, and compare O. LII. r. 3, 4. On appointment of receiver or manager on application of an unpaid creditor of a railway company, see *In re Manchester & Milford Railway Co., Ex parte Cambrian Railway Co.*, 14 Ch. D. 645.
(a) S. 25 (11), and see *Atherley* v. *Harvey*, 2 Q. B. D. 524.
(b) *Grant* v. *Holland*, 3 C. P. D. 180.   (c) S. 34.

(1). Where a plaintiff sues as administrator knowing that another claims to administer, and his letters of administration are afterwards revoked, he loses his costs (d).

(7). Where a defendant in another Division relies on an equity to set aside a deed, such Division has jurisdiction so far as is necessary to give effect to his defence (e).

(9). In such an action an Order for sale may be made under O. XL., r. 2 (f). The place and manner of the sale are in the discretion of the judge (g). And where the conduct of the sale is given by the Court to one person, whether a party or not, no other person may interfere (as by advertising without authority) (h).

11. Appeals from Inferior Courts lie to Divisional Courts, whose determination is final, unless special leave to appeal to the Court of Appeal be given by such Divisional Courts (i). This rule includes appeals from a County Court (j). Such appeal under the County Courts Act, 1875, s. 6, cannot be on a question of fact within the jurisdiction of the County Court as a Court of Common Law (k). It may be on a note *required* to be made at the trial of a point of law, or on a note made at the trial *without request*, but afterwards asked for by the appellant, but must not be on a note made subsequently to the trial (l). And a judgment may be upheld on appeal, not on the grounds given by the County Court Judge, but on other reasons which appear in his notes (m). The rule applies to a case reserved at Quarter Sessions (n), and to an application for a rule to Justices to state a case, such application to be made to the Queen's Bench

(d) *Houseman* v. *Houseman*, 1 Ch. D. 535.
(e) *Mostyn* v. *West Mostyn Coal and Iron Co.*, 1 C. P. D. 145.
(f) *Burnell* v. *Burnell*, 11 Ch. D. 213. See para. 81.
(g) *Macdonald* v. *Foster*, 6 Ch. D. 193.
(h) *Dean* v. *Wilson*, 10 Ch. D. 136.
(i) S. 45.
(j) *Crush* v. *Turner*, 38 L. T. 595.
(k) *Cousins* v. *Lombard Deposit Bank*, 1 Ex. D. 404 ; Cf. *Sharrock* v. *London and North Western Railway Co.*, 1 C. P. D. 70.
(l) *Seymour* .v. *Coulson*, 5 Q. B. D. 359, and *Pierpoint* v. *Cartwright*, 5 C. P. D. 139.
(m) *Chapman* v. *Knight*, 5 C. P. D. 308.
(n) *Reg.* v. *Swindon New Town Local Board*, 49 L. J. C. L. D. 522.

Division (o).   But an appeal lies *without special leave*
from refusal of rule to show cause why writ of *certiorari*
should not issue to bring up an Order to the Queen's
Bench Division from Petty Sessions (p).   And the Court
of Appeal has jurisdiction in questions of law arising upon
the records of the Mayor's Court (q), where there is error
on the record ; otherwise an appeal lies to a Divisional
Court, and from that only by special leave to the Court
of Appeal (r).   An appeal from a County Court (or *semble*,
other Inferior Courts) is not taken in Chambers (s).

12. No appeal lies from an Order made by the High
Court or a Judge (1) by consent, or (2) as to costs
only (t), except (1) by leave, (2) where such order is not
made in exercise of discretion and not accompanied by
any other direction (u), (3) where the Order imposes payment of costs within a given time as a condition of having
a new trial (v).

13. Orders made by a Judge at chambers not in the
exercise of his discretion may be set aside or discharged,
upon notice [Qu. of motion] by the Judge sitting in
Court or by any Divisional Court ; and this even where
consent has been given on behalf of a client by such
client's inadvertence, and he has afterwards withdrawn it,
but *secus* where he has changed his mind (w). But *semble*,
such discharge will be granted by a Judge in another
Division only where the Division to which the cause or
matter is assigned is not sitting (x).   No appeal from an
Order lies unless (1) such motion to discharge has been
made, or (2) special leave has been given by the Judge or
by the Court of Appeal (y).   But *semble*, a certificate in
the Order that the case has been fully argued before the

(o) *Ex parte Longbottom, Re Ellershaw*, 1 Q. B. D. 481.
(p) *Reg.* v. *Pemberton*, 5 Q. B. D. 95.
(q) *Le Blanch* v. *Reuter's Telegram Co.*, 1 Ex. D. 408.
(r) *Appleford* v. *Judkins*, 3 C. P. D. 489.
(s) *Williams* v. *Bindon*, W. N. 1876, 16, not following **Amies** v. **Clark**,
W. N. 1875, 230.
(t) S. 49. See para. 103, Pt. V.
(u) *Witt* v. *Corcoran*, 2 Ch D. 69.
(v) *Metropolitan Asylum District* v. *Hill*, 5 App. Cas. 582.
(w) *Holt* v. *Jesse*, 3 Ch. D. 177.
(x) *Campbell* v. *Fairlie*, W. N. 1880, 17.
(y) S. 50.

Judge at Chambers=special leave (z). But no appeal lies from an interpleader Order made at Chambers (a).

14. The Court or Judge may (1) by consent, or (2) in cases of prolonged, scientific, or local investigation, if convenient, at their or his discretion (b), on terms, at any time order any question or issue of fact or question of account, or of fact and account inextricably mixed (c), or any question which could be referred compulsorily to a Master under the Common Law Procedure Act, 1854, s. 3, or other issues accompanying a question of account (d), but not the action itself (e), to be tried by an Official or a Special Referee (f), whose report (unless set aside) is equivalent to a verdict (g). And with respect to proceedings before Referees and their reports, the Court or Judge has similar powers as with respect to arbitrators (h). In cases of arbitration, it is desirable that, where the award is made a rule of Court, submission to the arbitration should generally be made so also (i). Even an issue involving personal character may but rarely should be compulsorily referred (k).

15. No plaintiff who recovers a sum not exceeding £20 in an action in the High Court founded on contract or £10 if founded on tort, shall be entitled to costs unless (1) sufficient for bringing the action in the High Court is certified on the record, or (2) the Court or Judge allow costs, or *semble*, the relief sought exceeds the original jurisdiction of the County Courts (l.

(z) *Murr* v. *Cooke*, 34 L. T. 751.
(a) *Dodds* v. *Shepherd*, 1 Ex. D. 75. But see, *per contra*, *Witt* v. *Parker*, 25 W. R. 518 ; *McAndrew* v. *Barker*, 7 Ch. D. 701. See para. 26.
(b) *Saxby* v. *Gloucester Wagon Co.*, W. N. 1880, 28.
(c) *Ward* v. *Hall*, W. N. 1889, 69.
(d) *Ward* v. *Pilley*, 5 Q. B. D. 427.
(e) *Pontifex* v. *Severn*, 3 Q. B. D. 295 ; *Longman* v. *East*, 3 C. P. D. 142 ; *Braginton* v. *Yates*, W. N. 1880, 150.
(f) S. 57.
(g) S. 58.
(h) S. 59.
(i) *Jones* v. *Jones*, W. N. 1880, 133. Per Jessel, M. R.
(k) *Hoch* v. *Boor*, 49 L. J. C. L. D. 665.
(l) S. 67 embodying County Courts Act, 1867, s. 5. As to actions founded on contract and tort see *Pontifex* v. *Midland Railway Co.*, 3 Q. B. D. 23 ; *Fleming* v. *Manchester and Sheffield Railway Co.*, 4 Q B. D. 81. On the right of plaintiff and defendant respectively to costs of their successful issues, and as to general costs, see *Potter* v. *Chambers*, 4 C. P. D. 69, 457 ; *Neale* v. *Clarke*, 4 Ex. D. 286.

16. An action of contract, where the amount indorsed does not exceed £50 or is reduced to that sum by admitted set-off or otherwise, may on the application of the defendant within eight days after service, unless cause be shown to the contrary, be transferred to the County Court (*m*); and generally any action which might have been commenced in a County Court may be transferred thereto either (1) on the application of any party, or (2) by the Judge himself without any application (*n*); and in an action of tort on affidavit of the defendant that the plaintiff has no visible means of paying costs, the plaintiff may be called on to give security for costs or the action transferred to the County Court (*o*).

17. Inferior Courts, to the extent of their jurisdiction at Law, in Equity, and in Admiralty (*p*), may grant such relief and remedies as can be granted by the High Court, as *e.g.*, injunctions against nuisances, &c. (*q*), according to the rules enacted by the Judicature Acts (*r*); and therefore an Inferior Court has no power to restrain proceedings in the High Court (*s*). But where a defence or counterclaim exceeds the jurisdiction of an Inferior Court, (1) the plaintiff's case and the defence thereto only may be dealt with, or (2) on application by any party to the High Court or a Judge thereof, the proceedings may be transferred'to the High Court, and there carried on (*t*). And where judgment only is transferred under 1 & 2 Vict. c. 110 for execution, there is no jurisdiction to inquire into the proceedings in the Court below (*u*).

18. In the administration of insolvent estates and the winding up of companies (*v*) the same rules prevail as to the respective rights of secured and unsecured creditors,

(*m*) C. C. A. s. 7.
(*n*) Do. s. 8.
(*o*) D. s. 10.
(*p*) On Admiralty jurisdiction of County Court, see *The "Alina,"* 5 Ex. D. 227.
(*q*) *Martin v. Bannister*, 4 Q. B. D. 491.
r) Ss. 89, 91.
(*s*) *Cobbold v. Pyke*, 4 Ex. D. 315.
(*t*) S. 99.
(*u*) *Williams v. Bolland*, 1 C. P. D. 227.
(*v*) On practical extent of this rule, see Baldwin on Bankruptcy, and cases collected there, pp. 15, 16. Also *In re Westbourne Grove Drapery Co.*, 5 Ch. D. 248, 36 L. T. 489.

debts and liabilities proveable, valuation of annuities, and future and contingent liabilities, as in Bankruptcy (w). But an executor is not a secured creditor in virtue of his right of retainer (x).

19. Interlocutory and other proceedings in a cause or matter shall be taken generally in the Division to which such cause or matter is for the time being attached (y). Thus, an Order charging wilful default against an executor may, on proper case shown, be made during the progress of an administration action (z), but only where this is justified by the pleadings (a).

20. A cause or matter assigned to a wrong Division may (1), on summary application at any stage by motion on notice (b), be transferred or retained at the discretion of the Court or Judge (c), or (2) an action may be transferred from a Common Law to the Chancery Division, with the consent of the Lord Chancellor, by an Order at Chambers of any Common Law Judge, even one of another Division (d).

21. Forms and methods of procedure formerly in use and not otherwise provided for by the Acts or Rules may continue to be used (e), and where there was variance in the old practice between Common Law and Chancery, the more convenient one is to prevail (f).

(w) J. A. 1875, s. 10.
(x) *Lee* v. *Nuttall*, 12 Ch. D. 61, and see *Hodgson* v. *Fox, In re Hodgson*, 9 Ch. D. 673.
(y) J. A. 1875, s. 11 (1).
(z) *Job* v. *Job*, 6 Ch. D. 562.
(a) *Mayer* v. *Murray*, 8 Ch. D. 424.
(b) *Humphreys* v. *Edwards*, 45 L. J. Ch. D. 112.
(c) J. A. 1875, s. 11 (2), and see O. Ll. r. 1, 1 a, 2, 2 a, para. 117, 118.
(d) *Hillman* v. *Mayhew*, 1 Ex. D. 132.
(e) J. A. 1875, s. 21. See *Laming* v. *Gee*, W. N. 1878, 240.
(f) *Newbiggin-by-the-Sea Gas Co.* v. *Armstrong*, 13 Ch. D. 310.

PART II.

—◆—

WRIT.—CLOSE OF PLEADINGS.

1. An action in the High Court of Justice (*a*), including a suit formerly "commenced by bill or information in the High Court of Chancery" (*b*), is commenced by a Writ of Summons indorsed before it is issued (*c*), with a statement of the general (*d*) nature of the claim made (*e*), or of the relief or remedy required in the action, and specifying to which Division the action is intended to be assigned. The indorsement may, by leave of the Court or Judge, be extended by amendment (*f*) to include such substantial object of the action as an injunction or receiver (*g*); and if issued, as in an action by a creditor, "for self and others," this must be shown by the indorsement (*h*).

2. Subject to Rules of Court, proceedings and applications other than actions may be taken and made as under the old practice (*i*).

3. A. Where the plaintiff seeks merely to recover a debt or liquidated demand in money from the defendant on a contract or trust, the writ of summons (1) *may* be specially indorsed with the particulars of the amount,

(*a*) O. II. r. 1.

(*b*) *Attorney General v. Shrewsbury Bridge Co.*, W. N. 1880, 23.

(*c*) O. III. r. 1.

(*d*) O. III. r. 2.

(*e*) *Metropolitan Railway Company v. Defries*, 2 Q. B. D. 189, 387, 36 L. T. 494.

(*f*) O. III. r. 2.

(*g*) *Colebourne v. Colbourne*, 1 Ch. D. 690.

(*h*) O. III. r. 4, and *In re Royle, Fryer v. Royle*, 5 Ch. D. 540.

(*i*) O. I. r. 3, and as to what is or is not within the term "action," see *In re Phillips and Gill*, 1 Q. B. D. 278; *Delmar v. Freemantle*, 3 Ex. D. 287.

giving credit for any payment or set-off (*j*). *Semble*, the test of sufficiency of such particulars, is that they " enable the defendant to satisfy his mind whether he ought to pay or resist " (*k*). And the indorsement (2) *shall* state the amounts claimed respectively as debt or demand, and for costs, and further that proceedings will be stayed upon payment within four days after service, or time allowed for appearance where the writ is not for service within the jurisdiction (*l*).

B. In all cases of ordinary account, where the plaintiff desires in the first instance to have an account taken, the writ of summons *shall* be indorsed with a claim that such account be taken (*m*).

4. A writ of summons issued out of the Central Office shall be indorsed (*n*) with the address of the plaintiff, and (if suing in person) his occupation, and with the name, firm, or place of business of his solicitor (if any), and of the principal solicitor (if any) for whom such solicitor is agent, and if the place of business of such solicitor (or plaintiff suing in person) be more than three miles from Temple Bar with an " Address for Service " not more than three miles from Temple Bar. If the writ of summons is issued out of a District Registry there shall be, in addition to the plaintiff's and solicitor's (and principal solicitor's &c.) address, an " Address for Service " within the district [to which notice of appearance by the defendant shall be sent (*o*)], and where the defendant does not reside within the district, a second " Address for Service " not more than three miles from Temple Bar.

5. A concurrent writ (*p*) or writs may be issued, within twelve months after the issuing of the original writ, bearing *teste* of the same day as the original writ, sealed with the word " concurrent," and date of issue, to

(*j*) O. III. r. 6, Cf. O. LIII. rr. 2, 3, and as to what is a special indorsement, see *Parpaite Frères* v. *Dickenson*, 38 L. T. 178 ; *As on* v. *Hurwitz*, 41 L. T. 521.

(*k*) *Walker* v. *Hicks*, 3 Q. B. D. 8 ; *Smith* v. *Wilson*, 4 C. P. D. 392, 5 C. P. D. 25.

(*l*) O. III. r. 7.

(*m*) O. III. r. 8.

(*n*) O. IV. rr. 1, 2, 3a.

(*o*) *Smith* v. *Dobbin*, 3 Ex. D. 338.

(*p*) O. VI. rr. 1, 2.

be in force only so long as the original writ. A writ for service within, and a writ for service or whereof notice in lieu of service is to be given without, the jurisdiction may be concurrent (*q*). A writ shall only be in force for twelve calendar months including the day of date thereof, but may be renewed (*r*) by leave on good cause shown within twelve months, or even later (*s*), such renewal to be for six months, and so on from time to time, but no renewal can be allowed when the original writ has been lost (*t*).

6. A writ of summons (1) may be *served*, or (2) the defendant may by his solicitor agree to accept service and enter an appearance (*u*), in either of which cases the solicitor whose name is indorsed on the writ, may, by written demand, be called on to declare whether such writ was issued by him or with his authority or privity (*v*), and if such writ has been issued without the authority of the plaintiff, the plaintiff may serve notice on the defendant and on the solicitor, the action shall be dismissed, and the solicitor shall pay the costs of the plaintiff as between solicitor and client, and of the defendant as between party and party (*w*).

7. Service, wherever practicable, shall be personal (*x*), but leave on application supported by affidavit showing grounds (*y*) may be given for substituted or other service or notice in lieu of service on terms or as may seem just at discretion of the Court (*z*), as on a manager within the jurisdiction where the defendant is without (*a*), by post or otherwise with advertisement in the *London Gazette* or elsewhere ((*b*). But there can be no substituted service

(*q*) See *Beddington* v. *Beddington*, 1 P. D. 426.
(*r*) O. VIII. r. 1.
(*s*) *In re Jones*, *Eyre* v. *Cox*, 46 L. J. Ch. D. 316.
(*t*) *Davies* v. *Garland*, 1 Q. B. D. 250.
(*u*) O. IX. r. 1.   (*v*) O. VII. r. 1.
(*w*) *Newbiggin-by-the-Sea Gas Co.* v. *Armstrong*, 13 Ch. D. 310. *Nurse* v. *Durnford*, 13 Ch. D. 764.
(*x*) O. IX. r. 2.
(*y*) O. X.
(*z*) *Watt* v. *Barnett*, 3 Q. B. D. 183, 363, and see *Hartley* v. *Dilke*, 35 L. T. 706.
(*a*) *O'Neil* v. *Clason*, 46 L. J. Q. B. 191.
(*b*) *Cook* v. *Dey*, 2 Ch. D. 218; *Rafael* v. *Ongley*, 34 L. T. 124; *Caper* v. *Brewer*, 24 W. R. 40; *Whitley* v. *Honeywell*, 24 W. R. 851; *Crane* v.

where there is no person or corporation on whom original service could lawfully be made (c). Service on husband is good service on wife when both are defendants, unless otherwise ordered. Service on the father, guardian, or (if none) on the person with whom an infant resides, or who has care of the infant, and on a lunatic's committee or (if none) on the keeper of the asylum or other person in charge of him (d), or on the person with whom a person of unsound mind, &c. resides or under whose care such person is, shall be, unless otherwise ordered, good service. Where business is carried on in the name of a firm of more or apparently more than one person, service on one or more of the partners or at the principal place, within the jurisdiction, of the partnership business of any person having at the time of service the control or management of the partnership business there, shall be, subject to Rules of Court, good service on the firm or on the one person carrying on business in the name of the firm. But service on a director of a Company is not good service on the Company, if they keep a secretary (e). Service may be made in any manner provided by Statute for service on any body or number of persons, corporate or otherwise. In an action to recover land, service may, if necessary in case of vacant possession, be made by posting a copy on the door of the dwelling-house or other conspicuous part of the property (f). Indorsement of date of service shall within three days be made on the writ in case of personal but not of substituted service (g).

8. Service out of the jurisdiction of a writ upon a British subject, or notice upon a foreigner (h) or foreign corporation having no place of business in this country (i) [including a summons taken out by a liquidator under

Jullion, 2 Ch. D. 220 ; *Bellaby* v. *Grant*, W. N. 1876, 6 ; *Bank of White-haven* v. *Thompson*, W. N. 1877, 45 ; *Hamilton* v. *Davies*, W. N. 1880, 82.

(c) *Sloman* v. *New Zealand (Governor of)*, 1 C. P. D. 563.

(d) *Thorn* v. *Smith*, W. N. 1879, 81.

(e) *Lawrenson* v. *Dublin Metropolitan Junction Railway Co.*, W. N. 1877, 149.

(f) O. IX. rr. 3, 4, 5, 6a, 7, 8.

(g) *Dymond* v. *Croft*, 3 Ch. D. 512.

(h) Whether in Ch. or C. L. Division. *Padley* v. *Camphausen*, 10 Ch. D. 550.

(i) *Scott* v. *Royal Wax Candle Co.*, 1 Q. B. D. 404 ; *Westman* v. *Aktiebolaget Ekmans Mekaniska Snickerefabrik*, 1 Ex. D. 237.

a winding-up (*j*)] may be allowed at the discretion of the court or a judge, on an original party or third person (*k*), subject to the following conditions :—

A. Ground of action (*l*). 1. When the subject-matter is property situate within the jurisdiction (*m*), or any act (*n*), deed, will, or thing affecting such property.

2. When a contract made within the jurisdiction is sought to be enforced or rescinded, dissolved, annulled, or otherwise affected (*o*), or relief is demanded for the breach thereof (*p*).

3. When there has been within the jurisdiction a breach of a contract, wheresoever made (*q*).

4. When any act or thing sought to be restrained or removed, or for which damages are sought to be recovered, was or is to be done, or is situate within the jurisdiction.

B. Particulars (*r*). The application must be supported by affidavit, intituled, " In the [contemplated] action, and in the Judicature Act " (*s*), or otherwise by evidence showing (1) where the defendant may probably be found, (2) whether he is a British subject, (3) what are the grounds of the application (*t*).

C. Special Particulars as to A 2 and 3 (*u*). The judge in exercising his discretion shall have regard to (1) the

(*j*) *In re British Imperial Co.*, 5 Ch. D. 749.

(*k*) *Swansea Shipping Co.* v. *Duncan*, 1 Q. B. D. 644 ; *In re Luckie*, W. N. 1880, 12.

(*l*) O. XI. r. 1.

' (*m*) And therefore not below low-water mark : *Harris* v. *Owners of* " *Franconia*,' 2 C. P. D. 173.

(*n*) *i.e.*, physical act, not *e.g.*, a statement in the nature of slander of title, *Casey* v. *Arnott*,, 2 C. P. D. 24.

(*o*) *Tottenham* v. *Barry*, 12 Ch. D. 797 ; *Harris* v. *Fleming*, 13 Ch. D. 208.

(*p*) As to what is or is not such a breach, see *Creswell* v. *Prker*, 11 Ch. D. 601. For conflicting contracts within and without the jurisdiction, see *Norton* v. *Florence Land & Public Works Co.*, 7 Ch. D. 332. On conflicting jurisdiction of English and foreign courts, where both parties are in England, see *Buenos Ayres & Ensenada Port Railway Co.* v. *Northern Railway Co. of Buenos Ayres*, 2 Q. B. D. 210.

(*q*) Where one party is a foreign government, see *Twycross* v. *Dreyfus*, 5 Ch. D. 605.

(*r*) O. XI. r. 3.

(*s*) *Young* v. *Brassey*, 1 Ch. D. 277. Qu. whether evidence other than affidavit is admissible ?

(*t*) *Great Australian Gold Mining Co.* v. *Martin*, 5 Ch. D. 1.

(*u*) O. XI. r. 1a.

amount or value of the property; (2) the existence in Scotland or Ireland, if the defendant reside there, of a local court of limited jurisdiction having jurisdiction in the matter (v); (3) the comparative cost and convenience (w) of proceeding in England or in the place of the defendant's residence: which particulars, and such others as he may require, shall be stated in an affidavit.

The Order giving leave shall limit a time for appearance to a writ of summons or third party notice under O. XVI. r. 18 (x) according to circumstances (y), and may provide for service of interrogatories and issue of injunction applied for, *ex parte* (z). The Common Law form of notice in lieu of service is more convenient than the old Chancery form (a).

9. A defendant shall appear in London at the Central Office (b), unless the writ issues out of a district registry, when, if he neither resides nor carries on business within the district, he *may* (c), and, if he resides or carries on business there, he *must* (d) appear in the District Registry. Appearance shall be by delivery to the proper officer of a memorandum containing the names of all defendants in the case who appear at the same time, and by the same solicitor (e), and of a duplicate memorandum, to be sealed and returned as evidence of appearance (f). And where the defendant resides and is served without the district, notice of appearance, accompanied by the sealed duplicate, must be given or sent the same day to the " Address for Service " within the district (g). The rules as to place of business and " Address for Service " of a defendant ap-

(v) See *Woods* v. *McInnes*, 4 C. P. D. 67, 27 W. R. 49; *McPhail* v. *Lowder*, 48 L. J. Ch. D. 415.

(w) *Woods* v. *McInnes*, 4 C. P. D. 67; *Creswell* v. *Parker*, 11 Ch. D. 601; *Tottenham* v. *Barry*, 12 Ch. D. 797.

(x) *Swansea Shipping Co.* v. *Duncan*, 1 Q. B. D. 644.

(y) O. XI. r. 4.

(z) *Young* v. *Brassey*, 1 Ch. D. 277.

(a) *Bustros* v. *Bustros*, 14 Ch. D. 849.

(b) O. XII. rr. 1, 1a.

(c) Do. r. 3.

(d) Do. r. 2.

(e) Do. rr. 6 b, 13.

(f) Do. r. 6 b.

(g) *Smith* v. *Dobbin*, 3 Ex. D. 338. Rule 6 b, subsequent to this case, does not say which " Address for Service " is intended where there are two under O. XIV. r. 3a.

pearing in person or by a solicitor are similar to those which regulate the indorsement of a plaintiff's writ of summons (h). A defendant may appear at any time before judgment, but if after the time limited for appearance, is not, unless by leave, entitled to extension of time for defence or any other object (i).

A partner, whether sole or one of many, shall appear individually, but the subsequent proceedings continue in the name of the firm (j).

In an action for recovery of land, (1) a defendant in possession by his tenant shall so state in his appearance, but need not in his statement of defence plead his title, unless his right or some relief claimed by him is equitable (k) ; (2) a person not named in the writ may be let in by leave on application, supported by affidavit (l), to defend on appearance and notice; (3) any person may limit his defence to part of the property, as described with reasonable certainty in the memorandum of appearance, or in a notice to be served within four days after appearance (m).

10. On default of appearance, the plaintiff may file an affidavit of personal [not substituted (n)] service (o), or of notice in lieu of service; and further, if the defendant is an infant, or person of unsound mind, may apply for an Order appointing a guardian *ad litem*, supporting such application by proof of (1) service of writ, (2) *service* of notice of such application *after* the time for appearance and six clear days before the day named for hearing the application upon the person with whom or under whose care such defendant was at date of service of writ, or *leaving* such notice at such person's house, (3) unless dispensed with by leave of the Court or Judge, where an infant is not residing with or under the care of the father or guardian, service upon such father or guardian, or leaving at the house, as above (p) ; and thereupon—

(h) See O. IV. para. 4.
(i) O. XII. r. 15.
(j) Do. rr. 12, 12a.
(k) Do. r. 19 and O. XIX. r. 15.
(l) O. XII. rr. 18, 29.
(m) Do. r. 21.
(n) *Dymond* v. *Croft*, 3 Ch. D. 512.
(o) O. XIII. r. 2.   (p) Do. r. 1.

A. On a writ specially indorsed (q) may sign final judgment against such defendant or defendants as shall not have appeared (r) for debt or claim, interest up to date of judgment, and costs, subject to variation, as the Court or Judge may think just:

B. On a writ not specially indorsed, but claiming a debt or liquidated demand (s), may without delivering a statement of claim file an affidavit of service or notice and statement of particulars of claim, and after eight days enter final judgment for the sum indorsed and costs :

C. On a writ claiming goods and (unliquidated) damages or either of them (t), may without delivering statement of claim enter interlocutory judgment ; and the value of the goods and damages or either of them shall be ascertained by a writ of inquiry or otherwise, as the Court or a Judge may order:

D. In an action for recovery of land (u), may enter judgment for recovery of possession of the land [or of the part to which the defence of any defendant who has appeared does not apply], and may proceed as under A. B. or C. respectively on any further claim (if any) indorsed for mesne profits, arrears of rent, or damages for breach of contract (v):

E. In an action assigned by the Judicature Act, 1873, s. 34, to the Chancery Division, or not specially provided by the Rules in Order XIII. (w) may (1) after filing proper affidavit of service, and (2) after two clear days' notice of motion, set down the action on motion for judgment.

Where the writ has issued out of a District Registry, and the defendant having the option of appearing in the District Registry or at the Central Office in London has failed to appear (x) [or failed to send notice of appearance to the "Address for Service" in the district (y)], the

(q) O. XIII. r. 3.
(r) Do. r. 4.
(s) Do. r. 5.
(t) Do. r. 6.
(u) Do. r. 7.
(v) Do. r. 8.
(w) Do. r. 9.
(x) Do. r. 5a.
(y) *Smith* v. *Dobbin*, 3 Ex. D. 338.

plaintiff shall not enter judgment until after such time as a letter posted in London on the previous evening, in due time for delivery on the following morning, should have reached the defendant.

11. On appearance to writ specially indorsed, the plaintiff may, on affidavit made [but not necessarily before the granting of a summons to show cause (z)] by any person who can swear positively to the debt or cause of action, verifying the cause of action, and stating that in his belief there is no defence to the action, call on the defendant (a) [including a defendant corporation (b), but not a *feme covert* (c)] to show cause why the plaintiff should not be at liberty to sign final judgment, a copy of which affidavit shall accompany the summons or notice of motion returnable not less than two clear days after service (d). The defendant may show cause (e), (1) by offering to bring the sum into Court, which offer however does not carry the right to defend as of course (f), or (2) by affidavit, in reply to which the plaintiff may by leave file a counter-affidavit (g), but not as of right (h), or (3) "otherwise," and necessarily so where the defendant is a corporation (i). But the Court may still empower the plaintiff to sign judgment, if satisfied that a defence would be for the mere purpose of delay (j); or, on the other hand, if the defendant's affidavit gives grounds from which the Court may fairly conclude that there is a substantial defence, may give leave to defend unconditionally (k), or on such terms as to security or otherwise as seem just (l). And where the defendant has paid money into Court and then obtained final judgment of a Divisional Court, he is en-

(z) *Begg* v. *Cooper*, 40 L. T. 29.
(a) O. XIV. r. 1a.
(b) *Shelford* v. *Louth and East Coast Railway Co.*, 4 Ex. D. 317.
(c) *Ortner* v. *Fitzgibbon*, 43 L. T. 60.
(d) O. XIV. r. 2.
(e) Do. rr. 1a., 3.
(f) *Crump* v. *Cavendish*, 5 Ex. D. 211.
(g) *Davis* v. *Spence*, 1 C. P. D. 719; *Girvin* v. *Grepe*, 13 Ch. D. 174.
(h) *Rotheram* v. *Priest*, 41 L. T. 558.
(i) *Muirhead* v. *Direct United States Cable Co.*, 27 W. R. 708.
(j) *Lloyd's Banking Co.* v. *Ogle*, 1 Ex. D. 262.
(k) Do., and *Runnacles* v. *Mesquita*, 1 Q. B. D. 416.
(l) O. XIV., r. 6, and see *Ray* v. *Barker*, 4 Ex. D. 279; *Oriental Banking Co.* v. *Fitzgerald*, W. N. 1850, 119.

titled to return of the money, even though the plaintiff
has given notice of appeal (*m*). But where leave to defend
has been given, appeals are not encouraged (*n*). *Semble*,
not equally so, where leave is refused (*o*). Generally,
leave to defend is only refused where there is no doubt,
and the defendant has clearly not even a "plausible" defence (*p*). But where the defendant, without showing an
absolute defence, merely discloses facts deemed sufficient
to entitle him to defend, as *e.g.* raising a question whether
a release was by way of escrow (*q*), or that there are reasons for interrogating the plaintiff (*r*), the Court has discretion as to giving leave (*s*). And a claim to bring a
counter-claim does not necessarily carry with it leave to
defend (*t*).

Where the defendant sets up a defence as to part, the
plaintiff shall have judgment as to the undefended part on
such terms as the Judge thinks fit, and the defendant may
be allowed to defend as to the residue (*u*) without being
compelled to pay the part admitted to be due as a condition
precedent of being thus allowed to defend (*v*). And one
defendant having a good defence may be permitted, and
any other defendant, not having such defence, may not be
permitted to defend; in which case final judgment may be
entered and execution issued against the latter without
prejudice to the plaintiff's right of proceeding against the
former (*w*).

12. Where the writ is indorsed under O. III. r. 8 (*x*),
with a claim that account be taken, unless the defendant
appears, and by affidavit or otherwise satisfies the Court
or a Judge, that there is some preliminary question to be
tried, the Order for account shall be forthwith made (*y*)

(*m*) *Yorkshire Banking Co.* v. *Beatson* (2), 4 C. P. D. 213.
(*n*) *Papayanni* v. *Coutpas*, W. N. 1880, 109.
(*o*) *Wallingford* v. *Mutual Society*, 5 App. Cas. 685.
(*p*) *Beckingham* v. *Owen*, W. N., 1878, 215 ; *Thompson* v. *Marshall*,
W. N., 1879, 213. See also *Wallingford* v. *Mutual Society*, 5 App. Cas. 685.
(*q*) *Berridge* v. *Roberts*, W. N. 1876, 86.
(*r*) *Harrison* v. *Bottenheim*, 26 W. R. 362.
(*s*) *Ray* v. *Barker*, 4 Ex. D. 279 ; 48 L. J. (Ex.) 569.
(*t*) *Anglo-Italian Bank* v. *Davies*, 38 L. T. 197.
(*u*) O. XIV., r. 4.
(*v*) *Dennis* v. *Seymour*, 4 Ch. D. 80.
(*w*) O. XIV. r. 5.
(*x*) See para. 3   (*y*) O. XV. r. 1.

on application by summons after the time for appearance
has expired, supported by affidavit concisely stating the
grounds of claim to account (z), such Order to be so
made as not to prejudice the trial of issues which may
be raised by pleadings subsequently delivered (a). And
in such a case, matters on further consideration as to
costs may be proved by affidavit (b).

13. All persons may be joined as plaintiffs *in* whom
the right to any relief claimed, and as defendants *against*
whom any right claimed, is alleged to exist jointly,
severally, or in the alternative, (*semble*) where the subject
matter is sufficiently ascertained (c). *E.g.* an action for
libel may be brought jointly by persons not in partnership (d). And where two or more persons sue on a joint
claim, the defendant may set up against each individual
plaintiff separate counter claims sounding in damages (e),
but cannot, by way of counter claim, set up against a
third person a claim for relief in one only of two inconsistent alternatives (f). But a plaintiff can join as defendant to his claim, a person against whom he prays
alternative relief inconsistent with that prayed against
the other co-defendant (g). Judgment may be given for
one or more of the plaintiffs, for such relief as he or they
may be found entitled to, without any amendment, and
against one or more of the defendants, according to their
respective liabilities, without any amendment (h). Unless
the Court shall otherwise direct, an unsuccessful defendant shall be entitled to costs occasioned by joining a co-
plaintiff who is not found entitled to relief (i). *E.g.*
where a married woman sues to recover separate estate,
and joins her husband as co-plaintiff instead of making
him a defendant, and the defendant takes this objection, the

(z) O. XV. r. 2.
(a) *Gatti* v. *Webster*, 12 Ch. D. 771.
(b) *Benney* v. *Elliott*, W. N. 1880, 99.
(c) Wilson's Judicature Acts, p. 187, quoted in *Smith* v. *Richardson*, 4
C. P. D. 116, and Cf O. XVII. r 1, para. 25.
(d) *Booth* v. *Briscoe*, 2 Q. B. D. 496.
(e) *Manchester, Sheffield, and Lincolnshire Railway Co.* v. *Brooks*, 2 Ex.
D. 243.
(f) *Evans* v. *Buck*, 4 Ch. D. 432.
(g) *Child* v. *Stenning*, 5 Ch. D. 695.
(h) O. XVI. rr. 1, 3.
(i) Do. r. 1.

plaintiff, though successful, may be ordered to pay her costs of pleadings delivered subsequently to the taking of the objection (*j*). And an unsuccessful defendant is not bound to pay costs occasioned by the plaintiff having joined other defendants who are successful (*k*).

A plaintiff may at his option join all or any of the persons severally, or jointly and severally, liable on any one contract (*l*).—*e.g.* he may join those only who are solvent, and need not join or give notice to the others (*m*). —and he may join two or more persons among whom he is in doubt from which he is entitled to redress (*n*), nor is it necessary that each of such defendants should be interested as to all the relief, or every cause of action included in such action; but the Court or a Judge may make such Order as may appear just, to prevent any defendant from being embarrassed or put to expense by any action in which he has no interest (*o*).

14. Subject to special Order of the Court or a Judge, parties beneficially interested may be sufficiently represented by trustees, executors or administrators (*p*), but this does not include an administrator *ad litem* in the administration of an intestate's estate, where there is a general administrator (*q*), and *semble*, how far the beneficiaries may be sufficiently represented by bare trustees in redemption and foreclosure actions, depends on the particular circumstances (*r*).

15. Married women may sue by their next friend (*s*), in which case the Court has discretion as to his giving security for costs at any stage (*t*). By leave of the Court or a Judge not granted on a petition of course (*u*), a

(*j*) *Roberts* v. *Evans*, 7 Ch. D. 830.
(*k*) *Child* v. *Stenning*, 7 Ch. D. 413.
(*l*) O. XVI. r. 5.
(*m*) *Lloyd* v. *Dimmack*, 7 Ch. D. 398.
(*n*) O. XVI. r. 6, and see *Honduras Inter-Oceanic Railway Co.* v. *Tucker*, 2 Ex. D. 301.
(*o*) O. XVI. r. 4, and see *Cox* v. *Barker*, 3 Ch. D. 359.
(*p*) O. XVI. r. 7.
(*q*) *Dowdeswell* v. *Dowdeswell*, 9 Ch. D. 294.
(*r*) *Mills* v. *Jennings*, 13 Ch. D. 649.
(*s*) O. XVI. r. 8.
(*t*) *Martano* v. *Mann*, 14 Ch. D. 419.
(*u*) *Noel* v. *Noel*, 13 Ch. D. 510. This seems to alter the old practice as stated in Daniell's Ch. Pr. p. 164.

married woman may sue or defend without her husband,
as *e.g.* where she is defendant, and her husband is the
plaintiff's next friend (*v*), giving security for costs not as
of course, but if required by the Court or a Judge (*w*).

Where she sues for recovery of separate estate in
Equity (*x*), or under the Married Women's Property
Act. 1870 (*y*), her husband should be a co-defendant.

16. An infant may sue by his next friend (*z*), who
(*semble*) will be the father if living and not having adverse
interest (*a*), and may defend by a guardian *ad litem*. A
next friend who refuses to appeal may be removed (*b*).
An Order for costs against the next friend is personally
final, unless the question be reserved (*c*). A lunatic may
generally sue by his committee ; and a person of unsound
mind by his next friend, but if found lunatic by inquisi-
tion *pendente lite*, the action may by leave be continued
by the committee (*d*). A lunatic may similarly defend
by his committee, and a person of unsound mind by
a guardian *ad litem* (*e*).

17. Any two or more partners may sue in the name
of their firm, and any two or more (*f*), or one carrying
on business in the name of a firm apparently consisting
of more than one person (*g*), may be sued in the name of
such firm. Where a writ is sued out in the name of a
firm, (1) the *defendant* may in writing call on the plaintiffs
or their solicitors to declare the names and residences of
all partners, in default of which declaration all proceedings shall be stayed upon terms (*h*) ; and (2) any *party*
to an action may apply by summons to a Judge for a
statement of the names of the co-partners in the plaintiff
or defendant firm (*i*). But the Order for such statement

(*v*) *Lewis* v. *Nobbs*, 8 Ch. D. 591.
(*w*) *Noel* v. *Noel*, 13 Ch. D. 510.
(*x*) *Roberts* v. *Evans*, 7 Ch. D. 830.
(*y*) *Hancock* v. *Lablache*, 3 C. P. D. 197.
(*z*) O. XVI. r. 8.
(*a*) *Woolf* v. *Pemberton*, 6 Ch. D. 19.
(*b*) *Dupuy* v. *Welsford*, W. N. 1880, 121.
(*c*) *Caley* v. *Caley*, 25 W. R. 528.
(*d*) *Green* v. *Pratt*, 41 L. T. 30.
(*e*) O. XVIII.
(*f*) O. XVI. r. 10.
(*g*) Do. r. 10a.
(*h*) O. VII. r. 2.   (*i*) O. XVI. r. 10.

cannot be enforced by attachment under O. XXXI. r. 20 (*j*). Where a judgment has been obtained against two out of three co-partners. this bars an action for partnership debt against the third (*k*).

18. One or more of numerous parties having the same interest in the same action as trustees, underwriters, shareholders (*l*), mortgagees (*m*), &c., may sue or be sued or be authorised to defend on behalf of all (*n*). Where a plaintiff so sues, it should be so stated in the title of the writ and in the indorsement of claim (*o*). The other members of a class, if fairly represented, will be bound by the judgment (*p*). The Court, if it seem fit, may appoint a person or persons to represent an heir-at-law, next-of-kin, or class to be afterwards ascertained, for the determination of questions of construction, the judgment on which shall bind the person or class thus represented (*q*) ; or may order proceedings up to any given point to be carried on without some particular party being represented (*r*).

19. Subject to the Judicature Acts and Rules, it is provided (*s*), in accordance with 15 & 16 Vict. c. 86, s. 42, that a plaintiff falling under any of the five following characters may have a decree without joining or serving notice on others having similar interest :— (1) An heir, next-of-kin, residuary devisee or legatee ; (2) a legatee interested in a legacy charged on real estate, or any other person interested in the proceeds of real estate directed to be sold ; (3) a *cestui que trust* under a deed or instrument ; (4) one interested in the protection of property pending litigation or in cases of the nature of waste ; (5) an executor, administrator, or trustee desiring a decree against any one legatee, next-of-kin, or *cestui*

(*j*) *Pike* v. *Keene*, 24 W. R. 322. See para. 58.

(*k*) *Kendall* v. *Hamilton*, 4 App. Cas. 504.

(*l*) See Daniell's Ch. Pr. p. 172.

(*m*) *Lake* v. *South Kensington Hotel Co.*, 11 Ch. D. 121.

(*n*) O. XVI. r. 9.

(*o*) *Fryer* v. *Royle*, 5 Ch. D. 540 : following *Warraker* v. *Pryer*, 2 Ch. D. 109, not following *Cooper* v. *Blissett*, 1 Ch. D. 691.

(*p*) *Commissioners of Sewers, &c.*.v. *Gellatly*, 3 Ch. D. 610.

(*q*) O. XVI. r. 9a, and see *Chester* v. *Phillips*, 4 Ch. D. 230.

(*r*) *Hobbs* v. *Reid*, W. N. 1876, 95.

(*s*) O. XVI. r. 11.

que trust for administration of the estate, or execution of the trusts (*t*).

The Court may, if it see fit, require parties to be added, or give the conduct of the suit to one, and may make such Order as to place the defendant on the same footing as to costs with all other parties having a common interest. Persons having a common interest but not being parties shall be served with notice of the decree, or of Order on further consideration (*u*), and be bound thereby, and may by an Order of course have liberty to attend, and may apply to the Court to add to the decree. Such service is to be made on infants or persons of unsound mind as is made in the case of a writ of summons (*v*). A creditor may not in an administration action without leave join any party other than the executor or administrator (*w*).

20. The Court or a Judge may, with or without application of either party, upon terms, at any stage, as at trial (*x*) or after decree (*y*), order parties to be struck out or added (*z*). A defendant may be struck out notwithstanding he has delivered his statement of defence (*a*), but leave to strike out one and amend does not carry leave to strike out another (*b*), nor does an Order for amendment enable the plaintiff to strike out a defendant whose interest has determined (*c*). Where a plaintiff sues for himself and other bondholders and one dissents, the dissentient should be made a party (*d*). The assignee of a defendant *pendente lite* may be added (*e*), but an officer of a corporation cannot be added merely for the purpose of discovery (*f*). Nor, where an action is rightly

(*t*) S. 42, rules 1 6.
(*u*) *In re Rees, Rees* v. *Gregory,* 49 L. J. Ch. D. 568.
(*v*) O. XVI. r. 12a.   (*w*) Do. r. 12b.
(*x*) *Kino* v. *Rodkin,* 6 Ch. D. 160.
(*y*) *Attorney-General* v. *Council of Birmingham,* W. N. 1880, 112.
(*z*) O. XVI. r. 13, and see *Val de Travers Asphalte Co.* v. *London Tramways Co.,* 40 L. T. 133.
(*a*) *Vallance* v. *Birmingham & Midland Land Investment Corporation,* 2 Ch. D. 369.
(*b*) *Wymer* v. *Dodds,* 11 Ch. D. 436.
(*c*) *Elam* v. *Vaughan,* W. N. 1879, 69.
(*d*) *Wilson* v. *Church,* 9 Ch. D. 552.
(*e*) *Kino* v. *Rodkin,* 6 Ch. D. 160.
(*f*) *Wilson* v. *Church,* 9 Ch. D. 552.

brought by a representative under O. XVI. r. 9 (*g*), can other representatives be added on the defendant's application merely to increase his security for costs (*h*). *Semble*, a person against whom the plaintiff claims no relief cannot be added on the defendant's application merely to enable such person as a party to set up a counterclaim (*i*). No one shall be added as plaintiff or next friend of a plaintiff without his own consent. And the proceedings against added defendants shall be deemed to begin only from the time when they are served with summons or notice (*j*). Application to strike out or add a party may be made before trial by motion or in general by summons (*k*), and at the trial, even during examination of witnesses (*l*), in a summary way (*m*). Where the party added is out of the jurisdiction, the writ should be amended by indorsement before service (*n*).

21. Marriage, death, or bankruptcy of a party, or devolution of an estate by operation of law or otherwise, shall not cause an action to abate or become defective, if the cause of action survive (*o*) in some person before the Court (*p*). Therefore, where an action in tort is brought against a defendant personally who dies *pendente lite*, but by shaping the allegations differently his personal representative may be rendered liable, leave to amend may be given so as to bring a person before the Court (*q*). A husband, personal representative, trustee, or other successor in interest may, if necessary, (1) be made a party or being one already be made a party in another capacity by an Order obtained *ex parte* and of course (*r*) to be

---

(*g*) See para. 18.
(*h*) *De Hart* v. *Stevenson*, 1 Q. B. D. 313.
(*i*) *Norris* v. *Beazley*, 2 C. P. D. 80, decided partly with reference to the then procedure on Bills of Exchange. But it is submitted that the above principle may still be upheld.
(*j*) O. XVI. r. 13.
(*k*) *Wilson* v. *Church*, 9 Ch. D. 552.
(*l*) *Ruston* v. *Tobin*, W. N. 1880, 19.
(*m*) O. XVI. r. 14.
(*n*) *Keate* v. *Phillips*, W. N. 1878, 186.
(*o*) O. L. rr. 1, 2, 3, and see *Twycross* v. *Grant*, 4 C. P. D. 40.
(*p*) *Eldridge* v. *Burgess*, 7 Ch. D. 411.
(*q*) *Ashley* v. *Taylor*, 48 L. J. (Ch. D.), 406.
(*r*) *Darcy* v. *Whittaker*, W. N. 1876, 17 ; *Middleton* v. *Pollock*, W. N. 1876, 250.

served, unless otherwise directed, on all necessary parties; or (2) may be served with notice on terms. And such Order for the disposal of the action may be made as seems just (s). The person served with an Order may apply to have it discharged or varied within twelve days after service, or after appointment of a guardian *ad litem*, where necessary (t). A sole plaintiff, on becoming bankrupt, cannot proceed with the action, but if one of his two trustees refuse to go on, the other may have an Order of course, making the co-trustee a defendant (u). Where a plaintiff makes default in pleading and then becomes bankrupt, notice of motion to dismiss for want of prosecution should be served on his trustee, who may have the option given him to come in and proceed with the action (r). A person may be appointed to represent the estate of a deceased insolvent and intestate plaintiff to enable the defendant to move for dismissal in default of prosecution (w). Where a sole plaintiff dies pending a suit against his trustee for breach of trust, his representatives may be allowed the benefit of a decree *without* being made parties (x). The death of a sole defendant is no obstacle to the appointment of an *interim* receiver, where advisable (y). An Order for inquiry may after the death of a sole petitioner be continued for the benefit of his representatives (z). Where a defendant dies before service of judgment had been effected on him, leaving no personal representative, an affidavit may be filed and notice served on the widow (a). Where an executor after a decree in favour of his testator and notice of appeal obtains an Order permitting him to continue proceedings, he becomes a substantive party and personally liable for costs (b). Where notice of trial is served on a defendant

(s) O. L. rr. 2, 4, 6, and for form of petition for Order, see Daniell's Forms, 3rd ed. p. 9 ; and as to effect of Statutes of Limitations, see *Bright* v. *Campbell*, W. N. 1880, 20.

(t) O. L. rr. 6, 7.

(u) *Jackson* v. *North Eastern Railway Co.*, 5 Ch. D. 844.

(r) *Wright* v. *Swindon Railway Co.*, 4 Ch. D. 164.

(w) *Wingrove* v. *Thompson*, 11 Ch. D. 419.

(x) *Stone* v. *Bennet*, W. N. 1876, 152.

(y) *In re Parker, Cash* v. *Parker*, 12 Ch. D. 293.

(z) *In re Atkins' Estate*, 1 Ch. D. 82.

(a) *Alforth* v. *Espinach*, 36 L. T. 367.

(b) *Boynton* v. *Boynton*, 4 App. Cas. 733.

who afterwards becomes bankrupt, notice of motion for judgment against the trustee who does not appear need not be filed (c). And where out of several defendants jointly and severally liable some become bankrupt, the action may proceed against the others, without making the trustees of the bankrupts parties, or serving them with notice (d). Where an Order *nisi* has been obtained charging stock of a judgment debtor, and it afterwards appears that he was dead before the Order was obtained, such Order cannot under these Rules be made absolute (e). Nor can the assignee of a creditor proceed with a winding-up petition; such assignment is bad for maintenance (f).

22. Where a defendant is added, unless otherwise ordered, an amended writ of summons or notice shall be served on him; and, if a previous statement of claim had been delivered, a copy of an amended statement of claim shall be delivered to him, either along with the service of the amended writ or notice, or within four days after appearance (g).

23. When defendants or plaintiffs and defendants together (h) claim to be entitled to contribution, indemnity, remedy, or relief over against a third person, or where it appears that a question in the action should be determined between the plaintiff, defendant, and a third person, or between any or either of them, on notice issued by leave and served on such person (i), a proper Order may be made (j), where, in the discretion of the Judge, it appears that it will not tend to prejudice or delay the plaintiff (k). It is not necessary that the whole question should be identical between the different parties (l). One defendant may defend as against the

---

(c) *Chorlton* v. *Dickie*, 13 Ch. D. 160.
(d) *Lloyd* v. *Dimmack*, 7 Ch. D. 398.
(e) *Finney* v. *Hinde*, 4 Q. B. D. 102.
(f) *In re Paris Skating Rink Co.*, 5 Ch. D. 959.
(g) O. XVI. r. 15.
(h) *Treleven* v. *Bray*, 1 Ch. D. 176.
(i) O. XVI. r. 18.
(j) Do. r. 17.
(k) *Bower* v. *Hartley*, 1 Q. B. D. 652, and compare *Ex parte Smith, In re Collie*, 2 Ch. D. 51 ; *Harry* v. *Darcy*, 2 Ch. D. 751 ; *Horwell* v. *London General Omnibus Co.*, 2 Ex. D. 365.
(l) *Benecke* v. *Prost*, 1 Q. B. D. 419 ; *Swansea Shipping Co.* v. *Duncan*, 1 Q. B. D. 644 ; *Bower* v. *Hartley*, 1 Q. B. D. 652.

plaintiff, and claim as against a co-defendant, and delivery
of such pleading is sufficient notice to such co-defendant (*m*), even without an Order to that effect (*n*).　Where
not so delivered, notice may be served on the co-defendant,
and time allowed for him to deliver any further pleading (*o*).
But such pleading (*i.e.* against a co-defendant alone) is
not a counterclaim, which must be against the plaintiff
alone or jointly with some other person (*p*).　Nor may
a co-defendant join a third person as an alternative to a
counterclaim (*q*).　But he may combine a defence, reply
to a counterclaim of a co-defendant, and new claim
against a co-defendant, (1) where all parties agree to have
it so tried (*r*), (2) *semble*, in other cases at the discretion
of the Judge (*s*).　*Semble*, a plaintiff in an action in one
Division cannot be served with a third party notice by a
defendant against whom another plaintiff claims the same
relief in another Division (*t*).　A defendant who is a
residuary legatee may apply for a third party notice to
join the executor as a party to the action (*u*).　Where
a third person is to be brought in for the determination
of a question in the action, before or at the time of
making the Order, the Court or a Judge shall direct
proper notice to be given by the plaintiff to such person,
and if made at the trial, the Judge may postpone such
trial (*v*).　Where a counterclaim is set up against others
besides the plaintiff, or any third person is brought in
by a defendant on his counterclaim, this shall be shown
by a proper addition to the title of the defence, and such
defence shall be delivered within the proper period (*w*).

24. A third party in default of appearance shall be
held to admit the validity of any judgment obtained by
the plaintiff against the defendant, and if he desires to

(*m*) *Furness* v. *Booth*, 4 Ch. D. 586.

(*n*) *Butler* v. *Butler*, 14 Ch. D. 329.

(*o*) *Steel* v. *Dixon*, W. N. 1880, 113.

(*p*) *Dear* v. *Sworder*, 4 Ch. D. 476 ; *Turner* v. *Hednesford Gas Co.*, 3 Ex. D. 145.

(*q*) *Central African Trading Co.* v. *Grove*, 48 L. J. (Ex.), 510.

(*r*) *Marner* v. *Bright*, 11 Ch. D. 394 n.

(*s*) *Bagot* v. *Easton*, 11 Ch. D. 392.

(*t*) *Associated Home Co.* v. *Whitehcord*, 8 Ch. D. 457.

(*u*) *Hunter* v. *Young*, 4 Ex. D. 256.

(*v*) O. XVI. r. 19, and see *The* "*Carlburn*," 5 P. D. 59.

(*w*) O. XXII. rr. 5, 6.

dispute the plaintiff's claim, he must appear within eight days (x) or other time limited (y), or later by leave upon terms. If he appears, the Court or Judge may, on the application of the party who issued the notice, give liberty to defend on terms, and direct as to pleadings, amendments, discovery (z), proceedings generally, and mode or extent in or to which such person shall be bound by the decision (a). But it is optional with such third person to come in and appear, and he is not entitled to call on the defendant to pay his costs (b). Whether such third person on becoming a party can himself bring in subsequent parties, *quære* (c).

25. In general a plaintiff or plaintiffs, jointly or separately (d), may unite in the same action and statement of claim several causes of action (e), (*semble*) where the parties are sufficiently ascertained (f), and it is not necessary that each defendant be interested in each cause of action (g), but the Court or a Judge, on or without application of a defendant, may order separate trials; or make other Order for separate disposal; for amendment (if necessary) of the writ, indorsement, or statement of claim; and for costs, wherever it appears that such causes of action cannot be conveniently disposed of together (h). Thus, claims by or against husband and wife may be joined with claims by or against either of them separately (i), and in case of antenuptial debts of the wife it is not necessary expressly to allege that assets have come

(x) O. XVI. r. 20.
(y) *Swansea Shipping Co.* v. *Duncan*, 1 Q. B. D. 644.
(z) *McAllister* v. *Bishop of Rochester*, 5 C. P. D. 194.
(a) O. XVI. r. 21.
(b) *Yorkshire Wagon Co.* v. *Newport Coal Co.*, 5 Q. B. D. 268; *Dawson* v. *Shepherd*, 49 L. J. Ch. D. 529, W. N. 1880, 110.
(c) It appears to be virtually settled in the affirmative. See cases referred to above (b), and others quoted therein.
(d) O. XVII. r. 6. See *Witham* v. *Vane*, W. N. 1880, 108.
(e) O. XVII. r. 1.
(f) Wilson's *Judicature Acts*, p. 187, quoted in *Smith* v. *Richardson*, 4 C. P. D. 116, and cf. O. XVI. r. 1, para. 13.
(g) *Cox* v. *Barker*, 3 Ch. D. 359; *Child* v. *Stenning*, 5 Ch. D. 695, 7 Ch. D. 413.
(h) O. XVII. rr. 1, 8, 9; and for examples, see *Bayot* v. *Easton*, 7 Ch. D. 1; *Mycock* v. *Beatson*, 13 Ch. D. 384; *Desilla* v. *Schunk & Co. and Fels & Co.*, W. N. 1880, 96.
(i) O. XVII. r. 4.

to the hands of the husband (*j*). And claims by or against an executor or administrator as such may be joined with claims by or against him personally arising with reference to the same estate (*k*). But such claims cannot be combined in a counterclaim as against an executor who sues only in a strictly personal character (*l*). Nor can claims by a trustee in bankruptcy, unless by leave, be joined with claims by him in any other capacity (*m*). Nor, along with an action for recovery of land, can any cause of action other than claims for mesne profits, arrears for rent, and damages for breach of contract, under which such land is held (*n*) be joined unless by leave (*o*) obtained before the issue of the writ (*p*), as *e.g.* a claim for a receiver (*q*). But an action for recovery of land does not include a foreclosure action (*r*), nor an action for "declaration of title" without claiming possession (*s*).

26. A defendant in any action and in any Division after service of a writ and before defence (*t*), on affidavit showing that (1) he claims no interest in the subject-matter the right whereto is alleged to belong to some third party, (2) he does not collude with such third party, (3) he is ready to bring into Court, pay, or dispose of the subject-matter as ordered (*u*), may apply for an Order calling on the plaintiff and third party to interplead. The decision of a Judge at Chambers in a summary manner is final under the Common Law Procedure Act, 1860, s. 17, and no appeal lies to a Divisional Court (*v*), but in other cases an appeal lies from an Order made on

(*j*) *Matthews* v. *Whittle*, W. N. 1880, 43.
(*k*) O. XVII. r. 5.
(*l*) *Macdonald* v. *Carington*, 4 C. P. D. 28.
(*m*) O. XVII. r. 3.
(*n*) Do. r. 2.
(*o*) See, for examples, *Cook* v. *Enchmarch*, 2 Ch. D. 111 ; *Whetstone* v. *Dewis*, 1 Ch. D. 99.
(*p*) *Pilcher* v. *Hinds*, 11 Ch. D. 905.
(*q*) *Allen* v. *Kennel*, 24 W. R. 815.
(*r*) *Towell* v. *Slate Co.*, 3 Ch. D. 629.
(*s*) *Gledhill* v. *Hunter*, 14 Ch. D. 492 ; not following herein, *Whetstone* v. *Dewis*, 1 Ch. D. 99.
(*t*) O. I. r. 2.
(*u*) See 1 & 2 Wm. IV., c. 58, s. 1.
(*v*) Do. s. 2. See *Dodds* v. *Shepherd*, 1 Ex. D. 75 ; *Williams* v. *Richardson*, 36 L. T. 505.

an interpleader issue, as from any other interlocutory Order, within twenty-one days to the Court of Appeal (*w*). And an appeal lies from the refusal of an interpleader Order (*x*). Pending the hearing of an interpleader summons the plaintiff may issue a writ and the defendant may undertake to appear (*y*).

27. Every pleading shall state concisely material facts, and if to support distinct claims then separately and distinctly, but not evidence (*z*), as admissions (*a*), or proof that a person is heir-at-law to one deceased (*b*). It shall be delivered between parties by delivery to the solicitor of a party who appears by a solicitor, or in default of appearance by filing (*c*), which also, in case of default, is sufficient delivery of notice of motion for judgment (*d*). But filing is not necessary for delivery of a summons (*e*) or statement of claim (*f*) personally served on a defendant who has not appeared. Non-appearance of a defendant does not necessarily imply that he dispenses with a statement of claim (*g*). A statement of claim or counterclaim shall state specifically the relief claimed simply or in the alternative, and may also ask for general relief (*h*). But a defendant in his counter-claim may not ask for enforcement of a judgment in another Division, or in the alternative for other relief (*i*). *Semble*, no distinction can be made, as to effect, between " Set-off" and " Counterclaim " (*j*).

(*w*) *McAndrew* v. *Barker*, 7 Ch. D. 701.

(*x*) See *Attenborough* v. *London & St. Katharine's Dock Co.*, 3 C. P. D. 450.

(*y*) *Hooke* v. *Ind, Coope, & Co.*, 36 L. T. 467.

(*z*) O. XIX. rr. 4, 9.

(*a*) *Davy* v. *Garrett*, 7 Ch. D. 473.

(*b*) *Evelyn* v. *Evelyn*, W. N. 1880, 62.

(*c*) O. XIX. r. 6.

(*d*) *Morton* v. *Miller* (C. A.), 3 Ch. D. 516 ; and see *Dymond* v. *Croft*, 3 Ch. D. 512 ; not following *Cook* v. *Dey*, 2 Ch. D. 218.

(*e*) *Whitaker* v. *Thurston*, W. N. 1876, 232.

(*f*) *Renshaw* v. *Renshaw*, W. N. 1880, 7.

(*g*) *Minton* v. *Metcalf*, 46 L. J. Ch. D. 488 ; and see O. XIII. r. 9, para. 10.

(*h*) O. XIX. r. 8, and as to counterclaim see *Holloway* v. *York*, 25 W. R. 627.

(*i*) *Birmingham Estates Co.* v. *Smith*, 13 Ch. D. 506.

(*j*) *Neale* v. *Clarke*, 4 Ex. D. 286 ; *Cole* v. *Firth*, 4 Ex. D. 301 ; *Maples* v. *Masini*, 5 Q. B. D. 144.

28. A defendant may set up as counterclaim any right
or claim sounding in damages or not (k), subject to refusal
of permission to prosecute such counterclaim if, on the
plaintiff's application (l) at any time before reply (m), the
Court or Judge in their or his discretion (n) consider
that it cannot be conveniently disposed of in the pending
action, or ought not to be allowed, as being e.g. not sufficiently connected with the original subject-matter, or as
calculated unduly to embarrass and delay the plaintiff (o).
And the Court of Appeal will only in very strong cases
interfere with such discretion of the Court or Judge (p).
Unless by leave, a counterclaim must be confined to
facts existing at the date of issue of the writ (q); otherwise, on the plaintiff's summons, it may be struck out (r).
A counterclaim can only be brought where an action
could be brought (s), and cannot be continued after the
principal action is discontinued (t). And where both
claim and counterclaim are dismissed with costs, as a
rule, the plaintiff must pay the general costs, and the
defendant pay the amount by which the counterclaim has
increased the plaintiff's costs (u). A counterclaim may,
under some circumstances, set off against an assignee
damages due from the assignor (v). But this does not
include a liability incurred by the assignee of a policy
subsequent to its assignment, in cases falling under the
Policies of Marine Insurance Act 1868 (w). A husband
and wife joined as defendants in respect of her separate
estate may raise a counterclaim concerning chattels of

(k) O. XIX. r. 3.
(l) Can a Judge *mero motu*, without application of the plaintiff, reject a
counterclaim, e.g. as rendering the case "untriable"? The point does not
appear to have arisen, and something may be said for either view.
(m) O. XXII. r. 9.
(n) *Thompson* v. *Woodfine*, 38 L. T. 753; *Naylor* v. *Farrer*, 26 W. R.
809.
(o) *Padwick* v. *Scott*, 2 Ch. D. 736.
(p) *Huggons* v. *Tweed*, 10 Ch. D. 359.
(q) *Original Hartlepool Collieries* v. *Gibb*, 5 Ch. D. 713.
(r) *Ellis* v. *Munson*, W. N. 1876, 253.
(s) *Birmingham Estates Co.* v. *Smith*, 13 Ch. D. 506.
(t) *Varassour* v. *Krupp*, W. N. 1880, 11.
(u) *Saner* v. *Bilton*, 11 Ch. D. 416; and see *Mason* v. *Brentini*, W. N.
1880, 107, 144.
(v) *Young* v. *Kitchen*, 3 Ex. D. 127.
(w) *Pellas* v. *Neptune*, 5 C. P. D. 35.

hers and others of his (*x*). A debt owing from the
estate of one deceased, but due only after his death, cannot be set off against one due to the deceased in his life-
time (*y*). A counterclaim which raises no new issue of
fact but merely relies on facts in the claim itself will not
let in fresh evidence (*z*). Where a counterclaim is estab-
lished judgment will be given on the balance whether in
favour of the plaintiff or defendant (*a*).

29. Any facts on which the defendant relies as supporting a right of set-off or counterclaim must be specifically stated as such in the statement of defence (*b*), but
it is not essential that there be a separate heading to
such counterclaim (*c*), nor is it necessary therein to " set
out " again facts already referred to in the statement of
defence (*d*). But if the statement of defence and counterclaim form one continuous document, it is not sufficient
that the facts relied on appear in the statement of defence,
if it is not made clear which particular facts therein are
relied on for the counterclaim (*e*). Where a counterclaim
brought in an Inferior Court concerns matters beyond its
local jurisdiction, such Court may entertain the counterclaim only up to the amount claimed by the plaintiff (*f*).

30. In any pleading in an action, other than a general
joinder of issue by reply or subsequent pleading if any (*g*),
every allegation of fact is taken as admitted by the
opposite party (not being an infant, lunatic, &c.), unless it
be expressly or impliedly (*h*), specifically not generally (*i*),
nor evasively (*j*), denied. Thus, either party must

(*x*) *Hodson* v. *Mochi*, 8 Ch. D. 569.
(*y*) *Newell* v. *Provincial Bank of England*, 1 C. P. D. 496.
(*z*) *Green* v. *Serin*, 13 Ch. D. 589.
(*a*) O. XXII. r. 10 ; and see *Staples* v. *Young*, 2 Ex. D. 324 : *Rolfe* v.
Maclaren, 3 Ch. D. 106 ; and see further as to cases in County Courts, *Blake*
v. *Appleyard*, 3 Ex. D. 195 ; *Potter* v. *Chambers*, 4 C. P. D. 69 ; *Chatfield*
v. *Sedgwick*, 4 C. P. D. 383, 459.
(*b*) O. XIX. r. 10.
(*c*) *Lees* v. *Patterson*, 7 Ch. D. 866.
(*d*) *Birmingham Estates Co.* v. *Smith*, 13 Ch. D. 506.
(*e*) *Crowe* v. *Barnicot*, 6 Ch. D. 753.
(*f*) *Davis* v. *Flagstaff Silver Mining Co. of Utah*, 3 C. P. D. 228.
(*g*) O. XIX. r. 21.
(*h*) Do. r. 17.
(*i*) Do. r. 20 ; and see *Harris* v. *Gamble*, 7 Ch. D. 877 ; *Benbow* v. *Low*,
13 Ch. D. 553 ; *Green* v. *Serin*, 13 Ch. D. 589.
(*j*) O. XIX. r. 22.

specifically deny (if he denies) that any other party claims
in a representative or other capacity, as executor, or
trustee, or trustee in bankruptcy. So too, if he denies
the constitution of a partnership firm (k), or terms of
arrangement between parties (l). A denial of a particular
fact and of circumstances generally is insufficient (m), and
a general denial accompanied by specific assertion of a
particular fact puts that fact alone in issue (n). A bare
denial of a contract is a denial of the making thereof, not
of its legality or legal sufficiency (o). And if the defendant
relies on the Statute of Frauds, he must plead such facts
as render the Statute applicable (p).

31. But it is sufficient to state the effect of a material
document, setting out precise words only where themselves material (q), as e.g. words alleged to be libellous or
slanderous (r) ; and to allege as a fact (1) malicious or
other particular condition of mind of a person, without
setting out the circumstances leading to the inference; (2)
notice to any person, without setting out its forms or
terms, unless material ; (3) a contract or relation or more
than one in the alternative where implied and not arising
from express agreement, without referring otherwise than
generally to letters, conversations or circumstances where-
from such contract or relation or alternative is implied ;
provided that any agreement be actually pleaded as a
substantive ground of action (s), and any equitable title as
a defence relied on (t). A presumption of law not
specifically denied by one party need not be alleged as a
matter of fact by the other (u). And the Court may
make an Order as to costs occasioned by prolixity in any
pleading (v) or by unjustifiable denial or non-admission in
a statement of defence (w).

(k) O. XIX. r. 11.
(l) *Thorp* v. *Holdsworth*, 3 Ch. D. 637.
(m) *Tildesley* v. *Harper*, 7 Ch. D. 403 ; 10 Ch. D. 393.
(n) *Byrd* v. *Nunn*, 7 Ch. D. 284 ; *Collette* v. *Goode*, 7 Ch. D. 842.
(o) O. XIX. r. 23.
(p) *Pullen* v. *Snelus*, 48 L. J. C. P. 394; *Clark* v. *Callow*, W. N. 1876, 262.
(q) O. XIX. r. 24.
(r) *Harris* v. *Warre*, 4 C. P. D. 125.
(s) *Noad* v. *Murrow*, 40 L. T. 100.
(t) *Sutcliffe* v. *James*, 40 L. T. 875.
(u) O. XIX. rr. 24, 25, 26, 27, 28.
(v) Do. r. 2.   (w) O. XXII. r. 4.

32. A. A statement of claim, where *necessary*, is to be delivered within six weeks after appearance, unless the time be enlarged by the Court or a Judge (*x*), or by consent in writing (*y*).

B. But it is *unnecessary* where (1) it is dispensed with by (i) the defendant, or (ii) the Court or a Judge, as may generally be done in " short causes" (*z*) ; or

(2) the defendant has made default in appearance in cases under O. XIII. rr. 3—8 (*a*) ; or

(3) the defendant has appeared to a writ specially indorsed, but has not obtained leave to defend (*b*) ; or

(4) the defendant has appeared to such a writ and obtained leave but, no further Order being given, a notice that his claim is as on indorsement is in that case sufficient (*c*).

C. It is *optional* (1) where the defendant has not appeared, at any time after issue of writ ; (2) where he has and has dispensed with it, at any time not more than six weeks afterwards (*d*) ; but where not required, if the delivery appear to the Court or Judge unnecessary or improper, costs may be disallowed (*e*), or other Order made (*f*).

It is desirable, though not absolutely necessary, that a statement of claim should be signed by Counsel (*g*).

33. A statement of defence or demurrer (*h*) (1) *is to be* delivered, where a statement of claim has been delivered, within eight days of such delivery or of the time limited for appearance, whichever falls last, unless the time be enlarged by the Court or a Judge (*i*), or by consent in writing (*j*) ;

(*x*) Under O. LVII. r. 6, para. 128 ; and see *Higginbotham* v. *Aynsley*, 3 Ch. D. 258.

(*y*) O. LVII. r. 6a.

(*z*) O. XXI. r. 1 (*a*), and see *Green* v. *Colsby*, 1 Ch. D. 693. But see contra, *Breton* v. *Muckett*, 33 L. T. 684 ; *Boyes* v. *Cook*, 33 L. T. 778 ; *In re Huckwell, David* v. *Dalton*, W. N. 1879, 86.

(*a*) See para. 10.

(*b*) O. XIV. r. 1a.

(*c*) O. XXI. r. 4.   (*d*) O. XXI. r. 1 (*b*).

(*e*) Add. R. of C., O. VI. (Costs) 18.

(*f*) O. XXI. r. 1 (*c*).

(*g*) *Duckitt* v. *Jones*, 33 L. T. 777.

(*h*) *Hodges* v. *Hodges*, 2 Ch. D. 112.

(*i*) O. XXII. r. 1.

(*j*) O. LVII. r. 6a ; and see *Ambroise* v. *Evelyn*, 11 Ch. D. 759, which

(2) *may* be delivered, though the defendant has dispensed with a statement of claim and none has been
delivered, within eight days after appearance (*k*), unless
the time is enlarged as above ;

(3) *may* be delivered, on leave to defend to a writ
specially indorsed, within the time (if any) limited in the
Order for defence, or (if none) within eight days after the
Order (*l*).

A reply to a counterclaim may be delivered by a party
within the same time as a defence (*m*), but such party
cannot counterclaim against the defendant (*n*).

34. Grounds of defence which arise after action brought
but before delivery of statement of defence may be pleaded
therein (*o*) [but not in a counterclaim, except by leave (*p*)],
and if they arise after delivery of statement of defence
only within eight days by leave in further defence (*q*).

Similarly, grounds of defence to counterclaim which
arise before reply thereto may be pleaded in reply without leave, or if they arise after reply or time limited
therefor in further reply by leave within eight days.
The plaintiff may confess any such ground of defence as
above made by the defendant, and may, unless otherwise
ordered, sign judgment for costs up to its pleading (*r*).
Such ground of defence may include bankruptcy of the
defendant and the fact that the property claimed was in
his order and disposition at the time of the bankruptcy (*s*),
or *semble* bankruptcy of the plaintiff (*t*), but not performance of covenants after action brought (*u*).

35. Where in an action brought to recover a debt or
damages, the defendant, after service of the writ and
before or at the time of delivering his defence, or later by

case being before the issuing of this rule, the defendant had committed a
" technical irregularity."

(*k*) O. XXII. r. 2.
(*l*) Do. r. 3.
(*m*) Do. r. 8.
(*n*) *Street* v. *Gover*, 2 Q. B. D. 498.
(*o*) O. XX. r. 1.
(*p*) *Original Hartlepool Colleries* v. *Gibb*, 5 Ch. D. 713.
(*q*) O. XX. r. 2.
(*r*) Do. r. 3.
(*s*) *Champion* v. *Formby*, 7 Ch. D. 373.
(*t*) *Foster* v. *Gamger*, 1 Q. B. D. 666.
(*u*) *Callander* v. *Hawkins*, 2 C. P. D. 592.

leave, has paid money into Court; this shall be pleaded in
the defence (*v*), even though the greater part of the
causes of action are therein denied (*w*), and the claim in
respect whereof such payment is made shall be specified
therein, but it is not necessary to specify how much is
paid in respect of which items (*x*). Such payment must
be made in the manner directed by the Chancery Funds
Act, 1872, and Rules 1874, and not lodged in a district
bank (*y*). If made before defence, notice of payment
shall be served upon the plaintiff (*z*). The money shall
be paid out to the plaintiff, or to his solicitor on the
plaintiff's written authority (*a*); and the plaintiff may
accept the same, if before defence, within four days after
receipt of notice, otherwise before reply, in satisfaction of
the cause of action, and shall then give notice to the
defendant, and may, if the sum is accepted as entire
satisfaction, tax costs, and, if not paid within forty-eight
hours, sign judgment for them (*b*). Even where the four
days have been waived, the taxation of costs may still
take place (*c*). But where the plaintiff has failed to give
notice within four days, but has afterwards accepted (*d*),
or where he has not accepted and the defendant has afterwards substantially succeeded as to the residue (*e*), the
costs will be in the discretion of the Court.

36. Within three weeks after the defence, or last of the
defences, unless the time be extended (*ee*), the plaintiff
may deliver a reply, either by (1) simply joining issue
and thereby traversing all material facts (*f*) in a defence
unaccompanied by counterclaim (*g*) or in a defence and

(*v*) O. XXX. r. 1.
(*w*) *Hawksley* v. *Bradshaw*, 5 Q. B. D. 302.
(*x*) *Paraire* v. *Loibl*, 49 L. J. Ch. D. 481.
(*y*) *In re Smith, Hutchinson* v. *Ward*, 6 Ch. D. 692 ; *Finlay* v. *Davis*, 12 Ch. D. 735.
(*z*) O. XXX. r. 2.
(*a*) Do. r. 3.
(*b*) Do. r. 4.
(*c*) *Hoole* v. *Earnshaw*, W. N. 1878, 227.
(*d*) *Langridge* v. *Campbell*, 2 Ex. D. 281 ; *Greares* v. *Fleming*, 4 Q. B. D. 226.
(*e*) *Buckton* v. *Higgs*, 4 Ex. D. 174.
(*ee*) O. XXIV. r. 1.
(*f*) O. XIX. r. 21.
(*g*) *Williamson* v. *London & North Western Railway Co.*, 12 Ch. D. 787.

counterclaim which pleads no new facts in its support (h) [but if the counterclaim does plead new facts, the plaintiff must deal specifically with them (i)]; or (2) combining traverse, confession, and avoidance, of different parts (j). A reply may introduce new matter within reasonable limits by way of set-off or controverting statements made in the defence, but it must not refer to independent documents, set up new claims, plead evidence or arguments, or state conclusions of law (k).

37. The defendant may join issue on the reply, but no subsequent pleadings are allowed except by leave given on terms, every such pleading to be delivered within four days after the last previous one (l. When the plaintiff has delivered no reply within three weeks and no notice of trial within six weeks and obtains no extension of time, the defendant may either give notice of trial or may apply to have the action dismissed for want of prosecution, but cannot after the three weeks and before the close of the six apply for such relief as he may be entitled to on admissions of fact in the pleadings (m).

38. Any party may demur to a pleading of the opposite party or to such part of a pleading as sets up a distinct ground of action, defence, set-off, counterclaim, reply &c. (n), but not to one paragraph taken alone where, if taken along with another, it makes up a sufficient ground of pleading (o). A writ specially indorsed and notice in lieu of statement of claim together form such a pleading as is capable of demurrer (p). A demurrer must state that the facts alleged do not show any ground of action, defence &c., to which the Court can give effect against the party demurring (q), and must state specifically whether it demurs to the whole or to what (if any) part

(h) *Hillman* v. *Mayhew*, 24 W. R. 485.
(i) O. XIX. r. 20.
(j) *Hall* v. *Eve*, 4 Ch. D. 341.
(k) *Williamson* v. *London & North Western Railway Co.*, 12 Ch. D. 787.
(l) O. XXIV. r. 3.
(m) *Litton* v. *Litton*, 3 Ch. D. 793.
(n) O. XXVIII. r. 1.
(o) *Nathan* v. *Batchelor*, W. N. 1876, 172.
(p) *Robertson* v. *Howard*, 3 C. P. D. 280.
(q) O. XXVIII. r. 1.

of the pleading, and also state some ground of law. But additional grounds may be raised *ore tenus* (r).

The defence of the Statute of Frauds cannot be raised on demurrer (s), but *semble* the defence of the Statute of Limitations may be, whether as an original ground (t) or an additional one *ore tenus* (u). A defendant may combine a demurrer to part and defence to part in one pleading (v) ; and, where he has not originally demurred, may do so in an amended statement of defence to an amended statement of claim (w). And a party may by leave (x), but by leave only (y), plead as well as demur to the same matter. Where the opposite party does not appear at the hearing, the Court *may* admit a demurrer without argument (z).

39. A demurrer may be set aside with costs as stating a frivolous ground or none (a). Where it is allowed on argument, the opposite party shall generally pay costs (b) but not necessarily, as where the plaintiff charges fraud against a demurring defendant (c). Where it is over-ruled, the demurring party shall generally pay costs (d), but any objection to the over-ruling Order may, without being introduced in the next subsequent pleading, be introduced in argument (e). Such over-ruling Order is not interlocutory so as to require special leave of the Court of Appeal for appeal beyond twenty-one days (f). When the demurrer is over-ruled, the demurring party may still plead on obtaining an order on terms (g) which is granted "almost of course" (h). Where a plaintiff

(r) O. XXVIII. r. 2.
(s) *Catling* v. *King*, 5 Ch. D. 660.
(t) *Noyes* v. *Crawley*, 10 Ch. D. 31.
(u) *Dawkins* v. *Lord Penrhyn*, 6 Ch. D. 318.
(v) O. XXVIII. r. 4.
(w) *Powell* v. *Jewsbury*, 9 Ch. D. 34.
(x) O. XXVIII. r. 5.
(y) *Hagg* v. *Darley*, 47 L. J. Ch. D. 567.
(z) *Turner* v. *Samson*, W. N. 1876, 163.
(a) O. XXVIII. r. 2.
(b) Do. r. 8.
(c) *Duckett* v. *Gover*, 6 Ch. D. 82.
(d) O. XXVIII. r. 11.
(e) *Johnasson* v. *Bonhote*, 2 Ch. D. 298.
(f) *Trowell* v. *Shenton*, 8 Ch. D. 318.
(g) O. XXVIII. r. 12.
(h) *Bell* v. *Wilkinson*, W. N. 1878, 3.

neglects to pay costs of an unsuccessful demurrer, he is liable to have his action dismissed (i).

40. Amendment may be made

A. *without leave*, (1) of the statement of claim once before reply or close of time limited therefor, or if no defence, within four weeks after the last appearance (j) : (2) of set-off or counter claim of defendant before reply or close of time allowed him for pleading to reply, or, if no reply, within twenty-eight days after defence (k). And the opposite party may (1) apply within eight days to have such amendment disallowed or allowed on terms as to costs (l), including security for costs if a new case is thereby raised (m), but how far an " entirely new case " is allowed, *quære* (n) ; (2) apply for leave to plead or amend his former pleading on terms as to time &c. (o). Where the defendant neither pleads nor amends, the amendments will be taken as admitted, and his original defence will stand as a defence *pro tanto* (p).

But where the plaintiff has amended his statement of claim, the defendant should deliver a new defence or amend, and so on, *toties quoties* (q).

B. *with leave*, at any stage of the proceedings, as at the hearing (r), but in general to be within fourteen days (s) and on application ordinarily to be by summons (t) —— of statement of claim, defence, or reply (u). *E.g.* a defendant may be allowed, on terms, to substitute a separate and amended defence in lieu of a joint one (v) without filing any affidavit of grounds, or to introduce particular

(i) *White* v. *Bromige*, 38 **L. T.** 314.
(j) O. XXVII. r. 2.
(k) Do. r. 3.
(l) Do. r. 4.
(m) *Northampton Coal, Iron & Wagon Co.* v. *Midland Wagon Co.*, 7 Ch. D. 500.
(n) See remarks of Jessel, M. R. on headnote to *Budding* v. *Murdock*, 1 Ch. D. 42, in *Re St. Nazaire Co.*, 12 Ch. D. 92.
(o) O. XXVII. r. 5.
(p) *Boddy* v. *Wall*, 7 Ch. D. 164.
(q) *Darling* v. *Lawrence*, 46 L. J. Ch D. 808.
(r) *Nobel's Explosives Co.* v. *Jones, Scott, & Co.*, W. N. 1880, 77 ; *Dallinger* v. *St. Albyn*, 41 L. T. 460.
(s) O. XXVII. r. 7.
(t) *Marriott* v. *Marriott*, 26 W. R. 416.
(u) O. XXVII. r. 1.
(v) *Cargill* v. *Bower*, 4 Ch. D. 78.

facts in addition to a general allegation (*w*). And amendment will generally be allowed, unless (1) the Court or a Judge is satisfied of the *mala fides* of the applicant, or (2) that the blunder has wrought injury to the other side not to be compensated by costs or otherwise (*x*). By amendment of the writ and claim an action may be turned into an information and action without prejudice to a pending motion (*y*).

C. *by the Court or a Judge* (*z*) ordering to be struck out or amended matter, including a whole pleading (*a*), as scandalous [*e.g.* irrelevant allegations of fraud (*b*)], prejudicial, embarrassing [*e.g.* statements in nature of demurrers (*c*), general statements of title (*d*)], or delaying fair trial, or on the ground that amendment is necessary to determine the real question at issue [*e.g.* the plaintiff's state of mind (*e*)]. A faulty pleading may be struck out, even though the opposite party has not specified to which particular portions he objects (*f*). Allegations will not necessarily be struck out because they appear inconsistent (*g*); thus, payment into court may be pleaded and the greater part of the causes of action denied (*h*). And a defence may state many facts which, taken together, constitute an equitable ground of relief (*i*). The Court of Appeal will very rarely interfere with the discretion of the Court or Judge (*j*), but may do so, even where a motion to strike out has been dismissed with costs in the Court below (*k*).

(*w*) *King* v. *Corke*, 1 Ch. D. 57.
(*x*) Per Bramwell, L. J., in *Tildesley* v. *Harper*, 10 Ch. D. 393.
(*y*) *Caldwell* v. *Pagham Harbour Reclamation Co.*, 2 Ch. D. 221.
(*z*) O. XXVII. r. 1.
(*a*) *Cashin* v. *Cradock*, 3 Ch. D. 376.
(*b*) *Blake* v. *Albion Life Assurance Co.*, 45 L. J. C. P. 663.
(*c*) *Stokes* v. *Grant*, 4 C. P. D. 25.
(*d*) *Phillips* v. *Phillips*, 4 Q. B. D. 127. *Semble*, any defence is embarrassing which a defendant is not entitled to use. Per Jessel, M. R., in *Heugh* v. *Chamberlain*, W. N. 1877, 128.
(*e*) *Roe* v. *Davies*, 2 Ch. D. 729.
(*f*) *Williamson* v. *London & North Western Railway Co.*, 12 Ch. D. 787.
(*g*) *Bagot* v. *Easton* (C. A.), 7 Ch. D. 1.
(*h*) *Hawksley* v. *Bradshaw*, 5 Q. B. D. 302. See also *Spurr* v. *Hall*, 2 Q. B. D. 615 ; *Berdan* v. *Greenwood*, 3 Ex. D. 251.
(*i*) *Heap* v. *Marris*, 2 Q. B. D. 630.
(*j*) *Golding* v. *Wharton Salt Works Co.*, 1 Q. B. D. 374 ; *Watson* v. *Rodwell*, 3 Ch. D. 380.
(*k*) *Davey* v. *Garrett*, 7 Ch. D. 473.

41. Where the plaintiff has made default in delivering a statement of claim, on application by the defendant to dismiss the action with costs for want of prosecution, an order may be made accordingly (*l*), after which a Master has no jurisdiction to extend time (*m*), but the Court has (*n*), and in lieu of an order for dismissal may make an order on terms for an extension of time (*o*) or such other as seems just, and this even though an Order for security for costs has been made and not abandoned by the defendant (*p*). Where the plaintiff has made default in pleading and then become bankrupt, notice of motion to dismiss should be served on the trustee in bankruptcy (*q*).

42. Where the defendant, or one out of several, has made default in delivering a defence or demurrer to a claim for

A. a debt or liquidated demand, the plaintiff may enter final judgment for the amount and costs (*r*) :

B. detention of goods and damages, or either, he may enter interlocutory judgment, and have the value and damages assessed (*s*) :

C. Similarly, he may deal with A. and B. combined (*t*) :

D. recovery of land, he may enter judgment that the person whose title is asserted shall recover possession and costs, and have the value of mesne profits (if claimed) assessed (*u*) :

E. any other remedy, he may, without notice of setting down (*v*), set down the action on motion for judgment (*w*) but so as to give two clear days' notice of such motion for

(*l*) O. XXIX. r. 1.
(*m*) *Whistler* v. *Handcock*, 3 Q. B. D. 83 ; *Wallis* v. *Hepburn*, 3 Q. B. D. 84 (*n*); *King* v. *Davenport*, 4 Q. B. D. 402.
(*n*) *Burke* v. *Rooney*, 4 C. P. D. 226.
(*o*) *Higginbotham* v. *Aynsley*, 1 Ch. D. 288.
(*p*) *Lagrange* v. *McAndrew*, 4 Q. B. D. 210.
(*q*) *Wright* v. *Swindon, Marlborough, & Andover Railway Co.*, 4 Ch. D. 164.
(*r*) O. XXIX. rr. 2, 3.
(*s*) Do. rr. 4, 5.
(*t*) Do. r. 6.
(*u*) Do. rr. 7, 8.
(*v*) *Gillott* v. *Kerr*, W. N. 1876, 116.
(*w*) O. XXIX. r. 10.

judgment itself (*x*). And where one of several defendants has made default, the action may be set down on motion for judgment against him either (1) at once, or (2) at the same time as against any other defendants who have delivered their defence (*y*).

43. Where default is made of any subsequent pleading, the pleadings shall be deemed to be closed at the expiration of the time limited for delivering such pleading (*z*), unless one or more out of several defendants have leave to extend the time for defence (*a*). And the statements of fact in the last previous pleading shall be deemed to be admitted (*z*). Where default is made as between one of the original parties and a third party subsequently admitted, on application by the opposite party for such judgment as upon the pleadings he is entitled to, such judgment may be ordered, or such other order as is necessary may be made (*b*). Where default in pleading has been made by the defendant, the plaintiff must give at least two clear days' notice, and even then, as a general rule, the case will only come on in its regular turn, unless the Court is satisfied that the notice was ample (*c*).

44. Any judgment by default may be set aside on terms as to costs or otherwise (*d*), and right of application to set it aside is not barred by lapse of time where no irreparable wrong would be thereby done to the plaintiff (*e*).

45. An action may be (1) wholly discontinued, or (2) partly withdrawn, by the plaintiff on notice in writing before receipt of the defence, or afterwards before any other proceedings taken, except interlocutory applications (*f*); and the plaintiff's discontinuance of the action discontinues any counter-claim (*g*), or appeal (*h*). The

(*x*) *Parsons* v. *Harris*, 6 Ch. D. 694.
(*y*) O. XXIX. r. 11.
(*z*) O. XXIX. r. 12.
(*a*) *Ambroise* v. *Evelyn*, 11 Ch. D. 759.
(*b*) O. XXIX. r. 13.
(*c*) *Roupell* v. *Parsons*, W. N. 1876, 61 ; *Hate* v. *Snelling*, do. p. 77 ; *Pearse* v. *Spickett*, do. p. 109.
(*d*) O. XXIX. r. 14.
(*e*) *Atwood* v. *Chichester*, 3 Q. B. D. 722.
(*f*) O. XXIII. r. 1.
(*g*) *Vavasseur* v. *Krupp*, W. N. 1880, 11.
(*h*) *Conybeare* v. *Lewis*, 13 Ch. D. 469.

plaintiff shall pay the defendant's taxed costs or costs occasioned by the part withdrawn (*i*), and if the plaintiff gives an undertaking as to damages and then discontinues, a reference may be directed as to the damages (*j*). Before or at or after the hearing or trial, the Court or Judge may order an action to be discontinued, or part of the claim to be struck out, upon terms as to costs, as to subsequent action, or otherwise (*k*); but not so where an arbitrator has found on a special case substantially for the defendant (*l*). Where an action is discontinued or partly withdrawn, the defendant may sign judgment for costs or part costs (*m*).

46. A defendant cannot without leave withdraw his defence wholly or partly, but may by leave on application, upon terms in the discretion of the Court or a Judge (*n*), as *e.g.* on payment by the defendant of costs occasioned by his defence and by the plaintiff of an adjournment made into Court (*o*).

A cause entered for trial may be withdrawn by either party, on production of consent in writing signed by both (*p*).

(*i*) O. XXIII. r. 1.
(*j*) *Newcomen* v *Coulson*, 7 Ch. D. 764.
(*k*) O. XXIII. r. 1.
(*l*) *Stahlschmidt* v. *Walford*, 4 Q. B. D. 217.
(*m*) O. XXIII. r. 2a.
(*n*) O. XXIII. r. 1.
(*o*) *Real and Personal Advance Co.* v. *McCarthy*, 14 Ch. D. 188.
(*p*) O. XXIII. r. 2.

PART III.

47. Interrogatories in writing may be delivered.—
A. *without leave*, once :
(1) by the plaintiff at any time from delivery of his statement of claim to the close of the pleadings, both inclusive (*a*). But *semble*, in the Chancery Division a plaintiff may safely deliver interrogatories before delivery of a statement of defence ; in the Common Law Divisions he may even along with his statement of claim, but at risk of having them struck out in the exercise of the Judge's discretion (*b*) ;
(2) by the defendant at any time from delivery of his statement of defence to the close of the pleadings, both inclusive. But *semble*, a defendant cannot generally, even if he apply for leave, interrogate before delivery of statement of defence (*c*) :
B. *with leave*, (i) a second time within the above periods ; (ii) at any time, even after delay, as *e.g.* after an action is set down for hearing, in which case the costs may be made costs in the cause (*d*). An application for leave must be supported by an explanation, but not necessarily by affidavit (*e*). Any opposite party or parties

(*a*) O. XXXI. r. 1.
(*b*) Compare *Mercier* v. *Cotton*, 1 Q. B. D. 442, and *Disney* v. *Longbourne*, 2 Ch. D. 704, with *Harbord* v. *Monk*, 9 Ch. D. 616, and *Hancock* v. *Guerin*, 4 Ex. D. 3 ; and see remarks on this last in *Union Bank of London* v. *Manby*, 13 Ch. D. 239.
(*c*) *Disney* v. *Longbourne*, 2 Ch. D. 704 ; *Hawley* v. *Reade*, W. N. 1876, 64 ; *Mercantile Mutual Insurance Co.* v. *Shoesmith*, do.
(*d*) *London & Provincial Maritime Insurance Co.* v. *Davies*, 5 Ch. D. 775.
(*e*) *Ellis* v. *Ambler*, 36 L. T. 410.

[therefore not including a co-defendant to a counter-claim (*f*)] may be thus examined by interrogatories, a note at the foot thereof stating which of them each party is required to answer.

48. If a corporation or unincorporated company or body is a party, an Order may be obtained at Chambers for interrogating some member or officer of such corporation &c. (*g*), who need not be made a party for this purpose (*h*). The Order will be granted if the Judge thinks him likely to have the information, apart from any question as to relevancy thereof (*i*). A member of a corporation may refuse to file an answer until the taxed costs thereof are paid (*j*), but an officer cannot object that his knowledge is derived from privileged communications made to him in his private capacity (*k*). *Semble*, an action may be stayed until a foreign sovereign or corporation has named a proper person to give discovery (*l*).

49. Interrogatories are exhibited subject to enquiry, which may be made at the instance of any party, and if found by the Taxing Master, Court, or Judge to be unreasonable, vexatious, or of improper length, the costs occasioned thereby shall be borne by the party in fault (*m*).

50. A. On application at chambers within four days after service of interrogatories, (1) they may be *wholly* set aside as unreasonable or vexatious, or (2), *particular* ones may be struck out as *scandalous*. The applicant must specify to which interrogatories he objects (*n*). The Court of Appeal in its discretion may disallow interrogatories which had been allowed by the Court below (*o*).

B. In the affidavit in answer, *particular* interrogatories

(*f*) *Molloy* v. *Kilby*, W. N. 1880, 105.
(*g*) O. XXXI. r. 4.
(*h*) *Wilson* v. *Church*, 9 Ch. D. 552 ; and see *Costa Rica (Republic of)* v. *Erlanger*, 1 Ch. D. 171.
(*i*) *Berkeley* v. *Standard Discount Co.*, 9 Ch. D. 643.
(*j*) *Berkeley* v. *Standard Discount Co.*, 12 Ch. D. 295.
(*k*) *Swansea (Mayor of)* v. *Quirke*, 5 C. P. D. 106.
(*l*) *Costa Rica (Republic of)* v. *Erlanger*, 1 Ch. D. 171.
(*m*) O. XXXI. r. 2.
(*n*) *Allhusen* v. *Labouchere*, 3 Q. B. D. 654.
(*o*) *Rowcliffe* v. *Leigh*, 6 Ch. D. 256.

may be objected to as *scandalous*, irrelevant (*p*), not *bonâ fide*, premature (*q*), or on any other ground (*r*).

C. Whether a Judge can now order an interrogatory to be struck out as " objectionable " *mero motu* and without any application (*s*), *quære* (*t*).

An interrogatory imputing indictable matter is not necessarily scandalous, but the party's remedy is not to answer it (*u*).

51. An affidavit in answer to interrogatories (in general to be printed, if exceeding ten folios) is to be filed within ten days, or further time as allowed by the Court or a Judge (*r*), but *semble* any interrogatory may be left unanswered by a party who objects to it on a point of law (*w*). If not answered, or answered insufficiently, the party interrogating may apply, [in general by summons (*x*)] for an Order requiring an answer, or further answer (*y*), and in the latter case specifying to which interrogatories, or parts of which such further answer is required (*z*), the answer to be by affidavit or *virâ voce*, as directed. *Semble*, where a Judge refuses such an Order at Chambers, an appeal therefrom cannot open up fresh objections (*a*). Subject to the discretion of the Judge, the *whole* of the answers to interrogatories is not compelled to be put in evidence (*b*).

52. On application *ex parte* (*c*) at any time during any

(*p*) For examples of what is or is not irrelevant, see *Mansfield* v. *Childerhouse*, 4 Ch. D 82 ; *Rowcliffe* v. *Leigh*, 6 Ch. D. 256 ; *Allhusen* v. *Labouchere*, 3 Q. B. D. 654 ; *Sheward* v. *Lord Lonsdale*, 5 C. P. D. 47 ; *Eade* v. *Jacobs*, 3 Ex. D. 335 ; *West of England Bank* v. *Nickolls*, 6 Ch. D. 613 ; *Saunders* v. *Jones*, 7 Ch. D. 435 ; *Johns* v. *James*, 13 Ch. D. 370 ; *Lyon* v. *Tweddell*, 13 Ch D. 375.

(*q*) See *Saunders* v. *Jones*, 7 Ch. D. 435.

(*r*) O. XXXI. r. 5a. (Nov., 1878); and see *Gay* v. *Labouchere*, 4 Q. B. D. 206.

(*s*) *Atherley* v. *Harvey*, 2 Q. B. D. 524.

(*t*) Compare original Rule 5 (last part) with amended r. 5a. ; and see remarks of Fry J., in *Cracknell* v. *Janson*, 11 Ch. D. 13.

(*u*) *Fisher* v. *Owen*, 8 Ch. D. 645.

(*v*) O. XXXI. rr. 6, 7, 8.

(*w*) *Smith* v. *Berg*, 36 L. T. 471.

(*x*) *Chesterfield Colliery* v. *Black*, W. N. 1876, 204.

(*y*) O. XXXI. r. 10.

(*z*) *Anstey* v. *North & South Woolwich Subway Co.*, 11 Ch. D. 439.

(*a*) *Church* v. *Perry*, 36 L. T. 573.

(*b*) O. XXXI. r. 23.

(*c*) *Hennessy* v. *Bohmann, Osborne & Co.*, W. N. 1877, 14.

action or proceeding, as *e.g. generally* on application of
the plaintiff *before* the defendant delivers his defence (d),
an Order may be made for production on oath by any
party [including a third person who has appeared pursuant
to notice (e), or a person who not being a party, has yet
the same or a connected title with one of the parties (f)]
of such documents relating to any matter in question as
the Court or a Judge shall think right, to be dealt with
as shall seem just (g). And where the plaintiff disobeys
such an Order, the action may be dismissed by the
Court (h). But an Order will not in general be made in
favour of the plaintiff *before* delivery of his statement of
claim (i), especially where the object of the action itself
is delivery or inspection (j). Where documents are
required for the purpose of a reference, the Judge, and
not the Referee, is the person to make the Order (k).
An affidavit of documents may be made by the next
friend of a person of unsound mind, or by some other
person acquainted with the facts (l).

53. An order for production cannot be refused unless
(1) *semble*, the Court or Judge consider it premature (m),
or (2) the documents are privileged, as *e.g.* documents of
title under certain circumstances (n), communications
from the plaintiff's solicitor or solicitor's agent (o), documents *bonâ fide* intended for instruction of a solicitor in a
contemplated action (p), letters in answer to inquiries by
a party's solicitor, with a view to anticipated litigation (q),
a doctor's report of an examination at the instance of a

(d) *Union Bank of London* v. *Manby*, 13 Ch. D. 239.
(e) *McAllister* v. *Bishop of Rochester*, 5 C. P. D. 194.
(f) *West of England &c., Bank* v. *Canton Insurance Co*, 2 Ex. D. 472.
(g) O. XXXI. r. 11.
(h) *Republic of Liberia* v. *Roye*, 1 App. Cas. 139.
(i) *Cashin* v. *Cradock*, 2 Ch. D. 140.
(j) *Republic of Costa Rica* v. *Strousberg*, 11 Ch. D. 323.
(k) *Rowcliffe* v. *Leigh*, 4 Ch. D. 661.
(l) *Higginson* v. *Hall*, 10 Ch. D. 235.
(m) *Union Bank of London* v. *Manby*, 13 Ch. D. 239. Per James, L. J.
(n) *Bustros* v. *White*, 1 Q. B. D. 423; *Owen* v. *Wynn*, 9 Ch. D. 29. As
to a plaintiff's title-deeds, where the presumption of law is in his favour, see
Egremont Burial Board v. *Egremont Iron Ore Co.*, 14 Ch. D. 158.
(o) *Bustros* v. *White*, 1 Q. B. D. 423.
(p) *Southwark & Vauxhall Waterworks Co.* v. *Quick*, 3 Q. B. D. 315.
(q) *M'Corquodale* v. *Bell*, 1 C. P. D. 471.

party's solicitor (r), papers privileged in a former action (s), documents privileged on grounds of public policy, though *semble*, it should be stated in the affidavit *how* these last are so privileged (t). Though a defendant is not compelled to produce documents of title to land of which he is in possession, he is bound under Rule 12 to make an affidavit of them (u).

54. But confidential letters to a party's solicitor, *not* induced by inquiries (v), correspondence between vendor and vendee, relative to subject-matter of anticipated action by a sub-vendee (w), letters (under some circumstances) from defendant's unprofessional agent to defendant, relative to the subject matter of an action (x), communications between an officer of the Heralds' College and his "client" (y), and *semble* an agreement of compromise between the defendant and a third person relative to the subject-matter of an action (z) are not privileged. No appeal lies from a Judge's decision as to privilege where the documents have been by consent submitted to him (a).

55. *On application* by any party without affidavit (b), an Order may be made by a Judge for discovery on oath by any other party, of documents relating to a matter in question, which are, *or have been*, in his possession or power (c). But within what limits discovery can be enforced of documents not *at the time* in the party's possession or under his control, *quære* (d). Proceedings cannot be stayed by the defendant in an action on a marine policy until the plaintiff has obtained an affidavit of documents from a person who is not a party, not under

(r) *Friend* v. *London, Chatham, & Dover Railway Co.*, 2 Ex. D. 437.

(s) *Bullock* v. *Corry*, 3 Q. B. D. 356 ; *Bacon* v. *Bacon*, W. N. 1876, 96.

(t) *Kain* v. *Farrer*, W. N. 1877, 266.

(u) *New British Mutual Investment Co.* v. *Peel*, 3 C. P. D. 196.

(v) *M'Corquodale* v. *Bell*, 1 C. P. D. 471.

(w) *English* v. *Tottie*, 1 Q. B. D. 141.

(x) *Anderson* v. *Bank of British Columbia*, 2 Ch. D. 644, explaining *Ross* v. *Gibbs*, L. R. 8 Eq. 522.

(y) *Slade* v. *Tucker*, 14 Ch. D. 824.

(z) *Hutchins* v. *Glover*, 1 Q. B. D. 138.

(a) *Bustros* v. *White*, 1 Q. B. D. 423.

(b) O. XXXI. r. 12. Can a Judge in his discretion require an affidavit ? See *Johnson* v. *Smith*, 36 L. T. 741.

(c) O. XXXI. r. 12.

(d) See case quoted under (c).

the plaintiff's control, and not within the jurisdiction (*e*). An Order for discovery will not in general be made *before* delivery of a statement of claim (*f*). The party against whom such order is made shall in his affidavit specify sufficiently (*g*) any documents which he objects to produce (*h*), and if on the ground of privilege, shall further state and verify the grounds (*i*). No affidavit will be admitted in contradiction, the affidavit of the party answering being conclusive, unless (1) from such affidavit itself, (2) from documents referred to therein, or (3) from admission in pleadings of such party, it appears that other relevant documents exist. The party seeking discovery, if dissatisfied, should exhibit interrogatories (*j*). No mere statement of belief that the other party has other documents will support an application for a further Order (*k*). Prolix affidavits of documents may be struck off (*l*). *Semble*, the Crown is entitled to discovery, but not bound to give it (*m*).

56. *Without application* to the Court or a Judge, any party may at any time before hearing give notice in writing to any other party to produce, for inspection and taking of copies, any document referred to in such other party's pleadings or affidavits. The party receiving such notice shall within four days (or two, if he has already set forth such documents in an affidavit as in para. 55) notify in writing a time within three days for inspection at the office of his solicitor, and state which (if any) and on what grounds he objects to produce (*n*). Any party not complying with such notice cannot put such document in evidence, unless he satisfies the Court of some sufficient cause for non-compliance (*o*). But *semble*, it is

(*e*) *Fraser* v. *Burrows*, 2 Q. B. D. 624. This case as fully reported does not go nearly so far as stated by Sir W. T. Charley (3rd Edition, p. 581) who refers on it to W. N. 1877, 76.

(*f*) *Cashin* v. *Cradock*, 2 Ch D. 140; *Davies* v. *Williams*, 13 Ch. D. 550, and compare remarks of Bacon V. C. with *Union Bank of London* v. *Manby* (C. A.), 13 Ch. D. 239.

(*g*) *Taylor* v. *Batten*, 4 Q. B. D. 85; *Fortescue* v. *Fortescue*, 34 1. T. 847.
(*h*) O. XXXI. r. 13.　　　　　(*i*) *Gardner* v. *Irvin*, 4 Ex. D. 49.
(*j*) *Jones* v. *Monte Video Gas Co.*, W. N. 1880, 87.
(*k*) *Welsh Steam Coal Collieries Co.* v. *Gaskell*, 36 L. T. 352.
(*l*) *Taylor* v. *Keily*, W. N. 1876, 139.
(*m*) *Tomline* v. *The Queen*, W. N. 1879, 99.
(*n*) O. XXXI. r. 16.　　　　　(*o*) Do. r. 13.

generally a sufficient cause for non-compliance of a plaintiff that the defendant required inspection before putting in a statement of defence (*p*). And a petition for inspection of documents connected with a lunatic's estate by one claiming under him, must be supported by affidavit showing *prima facie* title (*q*).

57. If any party after receiving a written notice to produce for inspection omits to notify a time for, or objects to, inspection, the party desiring it may apply to a Judge for an Order. If the documents are not referred to in pleadings or affidavits, or disclosed in an affidavit of documents, such application shall be founded on an affidavit showing, (1) what are the documents, (2) the party's right to inspect, (3) that they are in the possession or power of the other party (*r*). On objection made by a party to discovery or inspection, and made on oath, if on the ground that such documents tend to criminate him (*s*), the Court or Judge shall determine whether or not any issue or question should be determined first, and the question of discovery or inspection reserved (*t*).

58. On non-compliance with an Order to answer interrogatories, or for discovery or inspection, an Order may, in the discretion of the Court (*u*), be made on application by the party interrogating, &c., that (1) a plaintiff have his action dismissed, or (2) a defendant his defence (if any) struck out, or (3) that any such party be attached (*v*), or any party's solicitor who, after being served as above, has neglected without reasonable excuse to give notice to his client (*w*). But an Order for " ordinary account," where the writ was so indorsed, or for declaration of copartners, cannot be enforced by attachment under this Rule (*x*).

59. A party may admit

A. *The truth of a case*, wholly or partially, as stated

(*p*) *Webster* v. *Whewall*, W. N. 1880, 142.
(*q*) *In re Smyth* (a Lunatic), W N. 1880, 144.
(*r*) O. XXXI. rr. 17, 18.
(*s*) *Webb* v. *East*, 5 Ex. D. 108.
(*t*) O. XXXI. r. 19.
(*u*) *Hartley* v. *Owen*, W. N. 1876, 193.
(*v*) O. XXXI. r. 20.
(*w*) Do. r. 22.
(*x*) *Pike* v. *Keene*, 24 W. R. 322.

in any pleading of another party, (1) expressly (*y*), or (2) by implication, as *e.g.* of a minimum sum certified by his own agent (*z*), or of a sum not denied to have been received as stated in an affidavit put in by the other party (*a*).

B. *Documents*, " saving just exceptions." A party who, after written notice, unreasonably refuses or neglects thus to admit, shall pay the costs of proving such documents, and costs of proving shall generally not be allowed unless such notice has been given (*b*). But documents thus admitted are not evidence unless formally put in and marked by the Registrar (*c*).

60. Necessary inquiries or accounts, or additional accounts, (*d*) may be directed by the Court or Judge at any stage pending further questions to be tried in the ordinary manner (*e*), but cannot be prosecuted in a District Registry except by direction of the Court or a Justice of the Division (*f*), nor can such Order be made on a counterclaim before dealing with the original claim (*g*).

61. Evidence of witnesses at the trial of an action shall be *vivâ voce* and in open Court, unless

(1) By formal written (*h*) agreement between the parties [on behalf of an infant defendant sufficiently given by a guardian *ad litem* (*i*)], such agreement being equivalent to an agreement for trial by a Judge without a Jury (*j*); or

(2) If the Court or Judge have ordered that particular facts should be proved by affidavit, or that some affidavit should be read; or

(3) Where it is found necessary in the discretion (*k*) of

(*y*) O. XXXII. rr. 2, 3.
(*z*) *London Syndicate* v. *Lord*, 8 Ch. D. 84.
(*a*) *Freeman* v. *Cox*, 8 Ch. D. 148.
(*b*) O. XXXII. rr. 2, 3.
(*c*) *Watson* v. *Rodwell*, 11 Ch. D. 153.
(*d*) *Barber* v. *Mackrell*, 12 Ch. D. 534.
(*e*) O. XXXIII., and see O. XL. r. 11 ; *Turquand* v. *Wilson*, 1 Ch. D. 85 ; *Ramsey* v. *Reade*, 1 Ch. D. 643.
(*f*) *Irlam* v. *Irlam*, 2 Ch. D. 608.
(*g*) *Rolfe* v. *Maclaren*, 3 Ch. D. 106.
(*h*) *New Westminster Brewery Co.* v. *Hannah*, 1 Ch. D. 278.
(*i*) *Knatchbull* v. *Fowler*, 1 Ch. D. 604.
(*j*) *Brooke* v. *Wigg*, 8 Ch. D. 510.
(*k*) *Steuart* v. *Gladstone*, 7 Ch. D. 394.

the Court or Judge to order on terms that the evidence
of any witnesses be taken elsewhere upon oath, by interrogatories or otherwise, before an officer, commissioner,
examiner, or other such person, and filed (*l*), even
where such depositions (being evidence *de bene esse*) are
not in the handwriting of the examiner, but taken down
before other persons, and certified by the examiner to
have been read over and signed by the witness in his
presence (*m*). No Order shall be made under (2) or (3),
where it appears that the other party *bonâ fide* desires
the production of a witness for cross-examination, and
that he can be produced (*n*). Nor under similar circumstances can an affidavit used on a former occasion be
read at the trial (*o*). An examiner has no discretion to
admit, if objected to, (1) the public, or (2) a clerk or
agent of any of the parties who is to be subsequently
called (*p*). A commission may be ordered with costs
reserved, and without security (*q*).

62. Evidence upon any motion, petition, or summons,
may be given by affidavit; but either party may apply
for an Order of the Court or a Judge for attendance for
cross-examination (*r*). Evidence on the Equity side of
the Exchequer Division may be generally by affidavit (*s*),
but in all cases of disputed facts the presumption is that
it should be oral (*t*).

63. The plaintiff's affidavits shall be filed and a list
delivered within fourteen days after agreement, as in 61
(1), or within time agreed upon by the parties, or allowed
by a Judge at Chambers; the defendant's, within fourteen
days after such delivery, or &c., as above; and the plaintiff's in reply within seven days, &c. Affidavits in reply
shall be confined to matters strictly in reply (*u*), but may
(at least, in the Chancery Division) also confirm the

(*l*) O. XXXVII. rr. 1, 4.
(*m*) *Bolton v. Bolton*, 2 Ch. D. 217.
(*n*) *Banque Franco-Egyptienne v. Lutscher*. W. N. 1879, 183.
(*o*) *Blackburn Union v. Brooks*, 7 Ch. D. 68.
(*p*) *In re Western of Canada Oil, &c., Co.*, 6 Ch. D. 109.
(*q*) *Spiller v. Paris Skating Rink Co.*, 27 W. R. 225.
(*r*) O. XXXVII. r. 2.
(*s*) O. LXII. r. 1, and (Exch.) Rules of March 14, 1866, r. 3.
(*t*) *Attorney General v. Metropolitan Railway Co.*, 5 Ex. D. 218.
(*u*) O. XXXVIII. rr. 1, 2, 3.

plaintiff's evidence in chief (*v*). *Semble*, no further affidavits can be filed, except on terms of amending pleadings (*w*).

64. Statements as to belief with its grounds are only admitted in affidavits on strictly interlocutory motions (*x*), and not in such as, while interlocutory in form, finally decide rights of parties. But where a party in the Court below admits such evidence, he may be precluded from objecting to it before the Court of Appeal (*y*). Affidavits sworn before the partner of a local solicitor who has got up the evidence are inadmissible (*z*).

65. Within fourteen days (generally) after the time limited for affidavits in reply, notice in writing may be given to produce any deponent for cross-examination on his affidavit (*a*), and where such affidavit includes accounts, notice of the particular items for cross-examination must be given, whether the party to be cross-examined is merely an accounting party, or one who seeks to charge by his account (*b*). Unless the deponent is produced according to such notice, his affidavit shall not (except by leave) be read as evidence, but it cannot therefore be demanded that such affidavit be taken off the file (*c*). The attendance of the deponent can be compelled in the ordinary way by the party who has received such notice (*d*), Evidence by affidavit shall be printed (*e*), unless *semble* this is dispensed with by the consent of both parties (*f*).

(*v*) *Peacock* v. *Hooper*, 7 Ch. D. 648.

(*w*) *Roe* v. *Davies*, 2 Ch. D. 729. For former Chancery Rules as to filing new evidence, see Daniell's Ch. Pr., p. 784 (5th edition). On admission of further *vivâ voce* evidence in rebuttal, see *Bigsby* v. *Dickinson*, 4 Ch. D. 21 ; *Rogers* v. *Manby*, W. N. 1880, 106 ; and Taylor on Evidence therein referred to.

(*x*) O. XXXVII. r. 3.

(*y*) *Gilbert* v. *Endean*, 9 Ch. D. 259.

(*z*) *Duke of Northumberland* v. *Todd*, 7 Ch. D. 777.

(*a*) O. XXXVIII. r. 4.

(*b*) *Bates* v. *Eley*, 1 Ch. D. 473.

(*c*) R. 4 ; and see *Meyrick* v. *James*, W. N. 1877, 120.

(*d*) O. XXXVIII. r. 5.

(*e*) Do. r. 6.

(*f*) *Attorney-General* v. *Pagham Harbour Reclamation Co*, W. N. 1876, 94.

PART IV.

TRIAL.—EXECUTION.

66. TRIAL shall take place, unless otherwise ordered by a Judge,

(1) Where named in the statement of claim, or

(2) If no place be named by the plaintiff, in Middlesex.

And any Order as to place of trial made by a Judge may be discharged or varied by a Divisional Court (*a*). The trial and hearing shall be before a Judge, Judges, Judge with assessors, Judge and jury, or before an Official or Special Referee, with or without assessors (*b*). And any question or issue of fact, or of fact and law, arising in any cause, may be ordered to be tried by any Commissioner or Commissioners (*c*), including thereunder Judges of the High Court of Justice and the Court of Appeal, Serjeants-at-Law, or any of Her Majesty's Counsel, to whom such commission may be assigned (*d*). *Semble*, the plaintiff is bound by his election of one of the above modes of trial (*e*). *Semble*, no trial can, even by consent, be heard in private, except where (1) lunatics or wards of Court are concerned, (2) public trial would defeat the object of the action, (3) where the Court follows the practice of the old Ecclesiastical Courts (*f*).

67. Notice of trial may, whether evidence is to be by affidavit or not (*g*), be given by the plaintiff at any time

---

(*a*) O. XXXVI. r. 1.

(*b*) Do. r. 2.

(*c*) Do. r. 29.

(*d*) J. A. 1873, ss. 29, 37 : J. A. 1875, s. 8.

(*e*) *Lascelles* v. *Butt*, 2 Ch. D. 588. But see the effect of r. 5, as stated in para. 69.

(*f*) *Nagle-Gillman* v. *Christopher*, 4 Ch. D. 173.

(*g*) O. XXXVIII. r. 6.

after the close of the pleadings, or with the reply (h), if (semble) it close the pleadings, and the plaintiff is in a position to deliver two copies of the whole of the proceedings (i); and such notice may specify one of the above modes of trial. The notice shall state whether it is for trial of the action or of issues, and if in a Common Law Division, shall state the place and day for which the action is to be entered for trial (j), and, if in a Chancery action, may do so (k). A Vice-Chancellor is sufficiently described as "a Judge in Middlesex" (l). Ten days' notice shall suffice, unless (1) it be otherwise ordered, or (2) the plaintiff has consented to "short notice" of four days (m). The cause is to be entered, if in London or Middlesex, within six days after notice (n) at most, but, if not entered on the day [of] or day after giving notice by the party giving it, may be entered within four days by the other party, unless the notice has been countermanded by consent or leave on terms (o). If the notice be for trial in London or Middlesex, this shall be deemed to be for any day on which it may come on in its order (p); if elsewhere, then for the first day of the next assizes (q); and the action or issue may be entered by either party not less than two days before the commission day in the District Registry (or elsewhere, as provided), or with the Associate (r).

68. If the defendant desires a jury, he may give notice out of Court, without moving for an Order, within four days after service of notice of trial, or extended time, and need not specify on which particular issues of fact he grounds his right to a jury (s). Such right is absolute (t), except, and only except, where it appears desirable to the

(h) O. XXXVI. r. 3.
(i) *Metropolitan Inner Circle Railway Co.* v. *Metropolitan Railway Co.,* 5 Ex. D. 196.
(j) O. XXXVI. rr. 8, 8a.
(k) *Redmayne* v. *Vaughan,* 24 W. R. 983.
(l) *Harris* v. *Gamble,* 7 Ch. D. 877.
(m) O. XXXVI. r. 9.
(n) Do. rr. 10, 10a.
(o) Do. rr. 13, 14.
(p) Do. r. 11.
(q) Do. r. 12.
(r) Do. r. 15a.
(s) Do. r. 3 : and see *Powell* v. *Williams,* 12 Ch. D. 234.
(t) *Sugg* v. *Silber,* 1 Q. B. D. 362 (Patent Case); *West* v. *White,* 4 Ch. D. 631 (nuisance); *Bordier* v. *Burrell,* 5 Ch. D, 512 (ancient lights).

Court or Judge to direct a trial, without a jury, of questions or issues of fact, or of fact and law, such as under
the former practice could without consent be tried without a jury (u). The discretion of the Court or Judge in so
determining is rarely interfered with, perhaps never, unless a Judge has exercised his discretion because on a point
of law he held an opinion which the Court of Appeal
thinks wrong (v). But the Court or Judge has discretion
to refuse such an application by a *plaintiff* who has been
guilty of undue delay (w), or even where the *defendant* has
asked for a jury (x). A defendant has no absolute right
to a jury in actions proper only for the Chancery Division
(y), as *e.g.* cases of fraud (z), specific performance (a),
purely conveyancing cases (b), issues of fact in an action
to restrain a trade-libel (c), trade-name raising an inference of law from which the facts are inseparable (d), or
where only minor issues of fact are involved (e). Nor can
a Judge in the Chancery Division try a case with a jury (f),
but a Judge, even of the Chancery Division, may direct
issues of fact to be tried by a Judge and jury (g), or questions and issues of fact, or fact and law, to be tried by
Commissioners, or at London or Middlesex sittings (h);
and if arising in an action in the Chancery Division, the
Order for such trial shall state on its face the reason (i),
as *e.g.*, that the defendant desires it, and the Court
sees no reason to the contrary (j). And an action, as
well as a question or issue, may be so ordered to be tried,

(u) O. XXXVI. r. 26 ; and see on Judge's discretion, *Powell* v. *Williams*,
12 Ch. D. 234 ; *Holmes* v. *Hervey*, 35 L. T. 600 ; *Sykes* v. *Firth*, 46 L. J.
Ch. D. 627.
(v) Per James L. J. in *Ruston* v. *Tobin*, 10 Ch. D. 558.
(w) *Lloyd* v. *Jones*, 7 Ch. D. 390.
(x) *Wedderburn* v. *Pickering*, 13 Ch. D. 769.
(y) *Swindell* v. *Birmingham Syndicate*, 3 Ch. D. 127.
(z) *Back* v. *Hay*, 5 Ch. D. 235.
(a) *Pilley* v. *Baylis*, 5 Ch. D. 241 ; *Wood* v. *Kay*, W. N. 1879, 295 :
Sykes v. *Firth*, 46 L. J. Ch. D. 627.
(b) *Wedderburn* v. *Pickering*, 13 Ch. D. 769.
(c) *Thomas* v. *Williams*, 49 L. J. Ch. D. 605.
(d) *Singer Manufacturing Co.* v. *Looy*, 11 Ch. D. 656.
(e) *Spratt's Patent* v. *Ward & Co.*, 11 Ch. D. 240.
(f) *Warner* v. *Murdoch*, 4 Ch. D. 750.
(g) O. XXXVI. r. 27 ; and see *Clarke* v. *Cookson*, 2 Ch. D. 246.
(h) O. XXXVI. r. 29.
(i) Do. r. 29a.
(j) *West* v. *White*, 4 Ch. D. 631.

but, *semble*, not without statement of some further sufficient reason than the mere wish of the parties (*k*).   But no special Order stating the reason is necessary where, no place being named in the statement of claim in an action attached to the Chancery Division, such action is set down to be tried in the county of Middlesex (*l*).

69. Within four days after service of notice of trial, or extended time, where (1) no notice of trial by a jury has been given, or (2) in a case suitable for trial before Referees, the plaintiff or defendant may apply for an Order to change the mode of trial of an action (*m*), but not of such issues as may be compulsorily referred (*n*).   And on the application of the defendant, or of the plaintiff under some circumstances (*o*), the Court or a Judge may order different questions of fact, or mixed questions of law and fact (*p*), to be tried by different modes, or some before others (*q*).   On trial of a question of fact, only one counsel will generally be heard on each side (*r*).

70. If the plaintiff does not give notice of trial, the defendant (subject to exceptions under the Rules, as where the Court or Judge has discretion to order particular modes) may (1) give notice specifying the mode, in which case the plaintiff may claim trial by a Judge with jury (*s*); or (2) apply [in the Chancery Division generally at Chambers (*t*)] to have the action dismissed for want of prosecution, or for such other Order on such terms as may seem just (*u*).

71. When an action is called on for trial, if

A. The plaintiff only appears, he may, *semble*, without proving service of notice of trial (*v*), prove his claim, so far as the burden of proof lies on him (*w*):

(*k*) *Wood & Ivery v. Hamblett*, 6 Ch. D. 113.
(*l*) *Hunt v. City of London Real Property Co.*, 3 Q. B. D. 19.
(*m*) O. XXXVI. r. 5.
(*n*) *Ward v. Pilley*, 5 Q. B. D. 427.
(*o*) *Emma Silver Mine Co. v. Grant*, 11 Ch. D. 694.
(*p*) *Tasmania Main Line Railway Co. v. Clark*, 27 W. R. 677.
(*q*) O. XXXVI. r. 6.
(*r*) *Conington v. Gilliat*, 1 Ch. D. 694.
(*s*) O. XXXVI. r. 4.
(*t*) *Freason v. Loe*, 26 W. R. 138.
(*u*) O. XXXVI. r. 4a.
(*v*) *Chorlton v. Dickie*, 13 Ch. D. 162; referring to *Cockshott* v. *London General Cab Co.*, 26 W. R. 31.   (*w*) O. XXXVI. r. 18.

B. The defendant only appears, he is entitled, without proving service of notice of trial on him (x), to judgment dismissing the action, unless he has a counter-claim, which he must then prove so far as the burden of proof lies on him (y). But where an action abates, as where the plaintiff has gone into liquidation, *pendente lite*, and the trustee has not appeared, and there is no evidence of service of notice on him, the Order will be to strike out the action from the list (z).

72. Application may be made at assizes or in Middlesex, within six days after trial, or, *semble*, after the party hears of it (a), to set aside a verdict or judgment on default of appearance on terms (b), as *e.g.* on payment of costs of the day, where the defendant was not represented because his solicitor had overlooked the transference of the action (c), where the plaintiff was not prepared (d), where one side had trusted to expectation of a settlement of the dispute (e).

73. The trial may, if the Judge thinks it expedient, be postponed or adjourned upon terms (f), as *e.g.* payment of costs incurred by the action being in the paper, where it was adjourned on the application of a party to add other parties (g). At or after the trial, (1) judgment, including a Referee's report if adopted (h), may be directed by Order to be entered, or (2) the case may be adjourned for further consideration, or (3) leave may be reserved to move for judgment (i). But no motion for judgment is necessary where the Registrar has certified to the superior Court the result of a trial ordered to be tried in a County Court (j).

(x) *James* v. *Crow*, 7 Ch. D. 410; following *Ex parte Lowe*, 7 Ch. D. 160; not following *Cockle* v. *Joyce*, 7 Ch. D. 56.
(y) O. XXXVI. r. 19.
(z) *Eldridge* v. *Burgess*, 7 Ch. D. 411.
(a) *Michell* v. *Wilson*, 25 W. R. 380.
(b) O. XXXVI. r. 20.
(c) *Burgoine* v. *Taylor*, 9 Ch. D. 1. . . . On delay in application, see *May* v. *Head*, W. N. 1880, 26; *Wilkins* v. *Bedford*, 35 L. T. 622.
(d) *King* v. *Sandeman*, 38 L. T. 461.
(e) *Wright* v. *Clifford*, 26 W. R. 369.
(f) O. XXXVI. r. 20.
(g) *Lydall* v. *Martinson*, 5 Ch. D. 780.
(h) *Wallis* v. *Lichfield*, W. N. 1876, 130.
(i) O. XXXVI. r. 22a.
(j) *Scutt* v. *Freeman*, 2 Q. B. D. 177.

74. Where there is no preliminary question of law to be settled (*k*), a cause or matter, or question in a cause or matter, [but not the action itself (*l*)] may be referred to a Referee, who may, subject to Order, hold the trial as most convenient (*m*), enforce attendance by *subpœna* (*n*), but not commit or attach any person (*o*), and may submit any question to the Court, or state facts for the Court to draw inferences therefrom. The Court may require of him explanation or reasons, and remit the matter wholly or partially to him or another for re-trial or further consideration, or may decide the question referred to him on evidence taken before him with or without additional evidence (*p*). A motion to set aside or vary the judgment in such a case must be supported by affidavit or other evidence of what took place at the trial (*q*). But when the matter referred to the Referee is simply the amount of damages in an action, the report cannot be altered or varied, though it may be accepted wholly or partially, or wholly disregarded, or remitted for amendment (*r*). The appeal from an Order of compulsory reference made by a Judge at *Nisi Prius* or Assizes is to the Court of Appeal (*s*).

75. In the Common Law Divisions, an application for new trial must be made

A. to a Divisional Court of the Division to which the Judge belongs who tried the action (*t*),

(1) after trial of an action by a Jury (*u*), even though the case was originally attached to the Chancery Division (*v*), and whether the verdict has been given in the ordinary way, or a finding directed by a Judge on

(*k*) *Lascelles* v. *Butt*, 2 Ch. D. 588.
(*l*) *Pontifex* v. *Severn*, 3 Q. B. D. 295 ; *Longman* v. *East*, 3 C. P. D. 142 : *Brayinton* v. *Yates*, W. N. 1880, 150.
(*m*) O. XXXVI. r. 30.
(*n*) Do. r. 31.
(*o*) Do. r. 33.
(*p*) Do. r. 34 (March, 1879).
(*q*) *Stubbs* v. *Boyle*, 2 Q. B. D. 124.
(*r*) *Dunkirk Colliery Co.* v. *Lever*, 9 Ch. D. 20. But *quære*, whether this case would not be now covered by Rule 34 as enlarged !
(*s*) *Hoch* v. *Boor*, 49 L. J. C. L. D. 665.
(*t*) *Jones* v. *Baxter*, 5 Ex. D. 275. But see *Jenkins* v. *Morris*, 14 Ch. D. 674.
(*u*) O. XXXIX. r. 1.
(*v*) *Hunt* v. *City of London Real Property Co.*, 3 Q. B. D. 19.

facts as undisputed (*w*), or a nonsuit directed (*x*), or either refused (*y*) ;

(2) When the case has been remitted from the High Court to a County Court and tried by a Judge alone (*z*) :

B. to the Court of Appeal when the trial has been by a Judge [of the High Court] without a Jury (*a*), whatever be the particular ground of objection on which the application is founded (*b*). But the finding on a particular issue in an action commenced in the Chancery Division directed to be tried by a Judge alone (*semble*, if actually tried in a Common Law Division) is an interlocutory Order, and the proper course is to appeal (*c*). So, too, where the Jury are discharged after the opening of the trial, and the case is in fact tried by a Judge (*d*).

76. In the Chancery Division, where definite issues of fact have been settled at the commencement of the trial, and a Judge of the Chancery Division has found a verdict on a matter of fact, this is equivalent to an interlocutory Order, and application for a new trial must be made to the Court of Appeal within the time limited for appeal, *i.e.* twenty-one days (*e*). But where no such definite issues have been settled at the commencement, an appeal against a verdict on matters of fact as well as of law, including an application for a new trial (*f*), lies within a year (*g*). Where there is no such separate verdict on matters of fact, but the case is decided by a Judge as a whole, no application for a new trial can be made on the ground of improper rejection of evidence, but an appeal lies (*h*).

77. Application for a new trial shall be by motion to show cause, at the expiration of eight days, or so soon

(*w*) *Yetts* v. *Foster*, 3 C. P. D. 437.
(*x*) *Etty* v. *Wilson*, 3 Ex. D. 359.
(*y*) *London* v. *Raffey*, 3 Q. B. D. 6 ; *Davis* v. *Goodbehere*, 4 Ex. D. 215.
(*z*) *Davies* v. *Felix*, 4 Ex. D. 32.
(*a*) O. XXXIX. r. 1.
(*b*) *Oastler* v. *Henderson*, 2 Q. B. D. 575.
(*c*) *McAndrew* v. *Barker*, 7 Ch. D. 701, and see *Jones* v. *Baxter*, 5 Ex. D. 275.
(*d*) *Metropolitan Bank* v. *Heiron*, W. N. 1880, 132.
(*e*) *Krehl* v. *Burrell*, 10 Ch. D. 420.
(*f*) O. LVIII. r. 5a., March, 1879.
(*g*) *Lowe* v. *Lowe*, 10 Ch. D. 432.
(*h*) *Dollman* v. *Jones*, 12 Ch. D. 553.

after as the case may be heard, and when made to a Divisional Court, (1) if the original trial was in London or Westminster, shall be within four days, or on the first subsequent day on which the Court sits to hear motions; (2) if elsewhere, within seven days after the last day of sitting on the Circuit, or (if the last day falls during vacation or within a week before), within the first four days of the next following sittings (i).

78. Where, and only where, the Court thinks substantial wrong or miscarriage has been occasioned as to trial of an action, or as to part of the matter, a new trial as to the whole or such part may be granted on the ground of misdirection (j), or improper admission or rejection of evidence (k), but not on the ground of premature admission of evidence provided it has afterwards become actually admissible (l), nor of the discovery of new evidence unless it be nearly or quite conclusive (m), nor where, in a trial by a Judge without a Jury, the plaintiff considers that the Judge has misdirected himself or found against the weight of evidence (n). But where substantial miscarriage is alleged, the burden is on the other side to disprove it (o). A new trial may be ordered on any question in an action without interfering with the finding as to any other question (p). But whether as to one defendant without disturbing the verdict as to another *quære* (q). The Order to show cause shall be a stay of proceedings, unless the Court otherwise order (r), and a copy shall be served within four days (s).

79. In all cases not specially provided for by the Act or Rules, judgment is obtained by motion for judgment (t). But such motion is not necessary where by the Act or

(i) O. XXXIX. r. 1a., March 1879.
(j) *Jenkins* v. *Morris*, 14 Ch. D. 674. See *Phillips* v. *South Western Railway Co.*, 5 Q. B. D. 78.
(k) O. XXXIX. r. 3.
(l) *Faund* v. *Wallace*, 35 L. T. 361.
(m) *Anderson* v. *Titmus*, 36 L. T. 711.
(n) *Potter* v. *Cotton*, 5 Ex. D. 137 ; *Pannell* v. *Nunn*, W. N. 1880, 148.
(o) *Anthony* v. *Halstead*, 37 L. T. 433.
(p) O. XXXIX. r. 4.
(q) *Purnell* v. *Great Western Railway Co. & Harris*, 1 Q. B. D. 636.
(r) O. XXXIX. r. 5.
(s) Do. r. 2.
(t) O. XL. r. 1.

Rules it may be obtained in any other manner as, *e.g.* where the writ was specially indorsed, and the defendant has not obtained leave to defend (*u*) ; where the defendant not being an infant or person of unsound mind has failed to appear, and the plaintiff has filed an affidavit of service or notice (*v*) ; in certain cases where the opposite party has made default in pleading (*w*) ; where at or after the trial the Judge has directed judgment to be entered (*x*) ; in certain cases as to costs alone (*y*) ; where a cause has been ordered to be tried in the County Court (*z*) ; and *semble*, where an arbitrator (not being a Referee) has made an award final and conclusive on the parties to an action (*a*).

80. A. Where judgment has been directed to be entered *simply*, any party may apply to the Court of Appeal by fourteen days' notice (*b*) to set it aside on the ground (1) after trial by a Jury, that the Judge has caused the finding to be wrongly entered with reference to the finding of the Jury ; or (2) after trial by a Judge, that, upon the finding entered, the judgment is wrong (*c*).

B. Where judgment has been directed to be entered *subject to leave to move*, the party to whom leave is reserved shall set down the action on motion for judgment, and give notice within the time limited (if any), or within ten days, stating (i.) the grounds of motion, (ii.) the relief sought, (iii.) that the motion is pursuant to leave reserved (*d*).

C. Where judgment has *not* been directed by a Judge or Referee to be entered, the plaintiff may set down the action, and give notice within ten days ; in default of his so doing, the defendant may (*e*).

D. Where a *Referee* has directed judgment to be entered,

(*u*) O. XIV. r. 1.
(*v*) O. XIII. rr. 1, 2.
(*w*) O. XXIX. rr. 2—8, 13.
(*x*) O. XXXVI. r. 22.
(*y*) O. XXX. r. 4.
(*z*) *Scutt* v. *Freeman*, 2 Q. B. D. 177.
(*a*) *Lloyd* v. *Lewis*, 2 Ex. D. 7.
(*b*) *Foster* v. *Roberts*, W. N. 1877, 11.
(*c*) O. XL. r. 4.
(*d*) Do. r. 2.
(*e*) Do. r. 3.

any party may move on affidavit or other evidence (*f*) to set it aside on the ground that, upon the finding entered, the judgment is wrong (*g*).

81. Where issues or questions of fact have been tried or determined as ordered, the plaintiff or (in his default) the defendant after ten days may set down the action, and give notice (*h*). And where there has been trial of some only out of several such issues or questions, necessarily arising and not being merely hypothetical (*i*), the Court on application may, if expedient, give leave on terms to set down the action, and direct as to postponing the other questions (*j*).

82. No action shall, except by leave, be set down later than one year after the right to do so has accrued (*k*).

83. On motion for judgment or for new trial, the Court may, if satisfied that it has before it all necessary materials, and where there is no evidence to go to a Jury (*l*), give judgment (*m*), and may set aside a judgment given in a trial before a Jury (*n*); but will not, unless thus satisfied (*o*). If there has been notice of appeal, and an *ex parte* rule *nisi* for new trial not set down on the first notice, no fresh notice of appeal is necessary, but the party who gave the notice will be liable for costs thereof (*p*). The Court, if not satisfied, may direct the motion to stand over, and any issues, questions, accounts, or inquiries, to be tried, determined, taken, or made (*q*).

84. Any party at any stage after two clear days' notice (*r*) may apply by motion to the Court, or to a Judge, for such Order as he is entitled to on clear (*s*)

(*f*) *Stubbs* v. *Boyle*, 2 Q. B. D. 124.
(*g*) O. XL. r. 5.
(*h*) Do. r. 7.
(*i*) *Republic of Bolivia* v. *National Bolivian Navigation Co.*, 24 W. R. 361.
(*j*) O. XL. r. 8.
(*k*) Do. r. 9.
(*l*) *Brewster* v. *Durrand*, W. N. 1880, 27.
(*m*) O. XL. r. 10.
(*n*) *Hamilton & Co.* v. *Johnson & Co.*, 5 Q. B. D. 263.
(*o*) *Milissich* v. *Lloyds*, W. N. 1877, 36.
(*p*) *Waddell* v. *Blockey*, 10 Ch. D. 416.
(*q*) O. XL. r. 10.
(*r*) *Parsons* v. *Harris*, 6 Ch. D. 694.
(*s*) *Gilbert* v. *Smith*, 2 Ch. D. 686 ; *Chilton* v. *Corporation of London*, 7 Ch. D. 686.

admissions of fact in the pleadings (*t*), or on allegations of fact in a statement of claim evasively (*u*) or not specifically (*v*) denied in the defence; as *e.g.* for an Order for accounts of partnership (*w*), of trusts (*x*), of mortgage (*y*), for inquiry (*z*), or for sale in partition action (*a*) &c. Further consideration may be reserved (*b*). Notice of motion for a decree or decretal Order may be given, without setting down the motion (*c*), so soon as the applicant's right to the relief claimed has appeared from the pleadings. But not so moving is not necessarily a waiver of right to judgment on admissions (*d*). The relief may be given, in the discretion of the Court or Judge (*e*), on terms (*f*), as *e.g.* an Order *nisi* binding absent parties three days after service, unless they show cause (*g*). But default in delivering a defence (*h*), and default of pleading generally (*i*), do not make such an admission of fact, and general joinder of issue on a counterclaim, without specific denial of the statements therein, does not warrant an immediate Order (*j*).

85. On delivery of a copy of the whole of the pleadings, judgment shall be entered by the proper officer (*k*), and, if in a Common Law Division in London, at the Central Office (*l*), dated, where pronounced by the Court or a Judge in Court, as of the day whereon pronounced (*m*);

(*t*) O. XL. r. 11, and see *Lord Hanmer* v. *Flight*, 36 L. T. 279.

(*u*) *Thorp* v. *Holdsworth*, 3 Ch. D. 637.

(*v*) *Symonds* v. *Jenkins*, 34 L. T. 277; *Rutter* v. *Tregent*, 12 Ch. D. 758.

(*w*) *Turquand* v. *Wilson*, 1 Ch. D. 85.

(*x*) *Bennett* v. *Moore*, 1 Ch. D. 692.

(*y*) *Martin* v. *Gale*, 4 Ch. D. 428.

(*z*) *Gilbert* v. *Smith*, 2 Ch. D. 686.

(*a*) *Burnell* v. *Burnell*, 11 Ch D. 213. See for other examples, *Rumsey* v. *Reade*, 1 Ch. D. 643; *Jenkins* v. *Davies*, 1 Ch. D. 696; *Bridson* v. *Smith*, W. N. 1876, 103.

(*b*) *Bennett* v. *Moore*, 1 Ch. D. 692; *Gilbert* v. *Smith*, 2 Ch. D. 686.

(*c*) *Hetherington* v. *Longrigg*, 10 Ch. D. 162.

(*d*) *Tildesley* v. *Harper*, 7 Ch. D. 403.

(*e*) Per Jessel, M. R. in *Mellor* v. *Sidebottom*, 5 Ch. D. 342.

(*f*) O. XL. r. 11.

(*g*) *Wilson* v. *Church*, 9 Ch. D. 552.

(*h*) *Gillott* v. *Kerr*, 24 W. R. 428.

(*i*) *Litton* v. *Litton*, 3 Ch. D. 793.

(*j*) *Rolfe* v. *Maclaren*, 3 Ch. D. 106, and see *Fritz* v. *Hobson*, 14 Ch. D. 558, 562.

(*k*) O. XLI. r. 1.

(*l*) Do. r. 1a.   (*m*) Do. r. 2.

otherwise as of the day whereon the documents are left with the proper officer (n) after examination of any necessary affidavit or document (n), or production of Order or certificate (o). A Judge may not direct the entry of a judgment in disregard of and contrary to a relevant finding of a Jury (p).

86. A judgment of nonsuit, unless otherwise ordered, is equivalent to a judgment on the merits, but may be set aside on terms in case of mistake, surprise, or accident (q). Mere clerical mistakes and accidental slips or omissions may be corrected on motion without appeal (r), but a judgment by consent cannot after entry be varied for any mistake, except such as would suffice to set aside an agreement (s). On motion to set aside judgment, a Divisional Court may give judgment, if satisfied that they have before them all necessary materials (t).

87. Judgment for, A., recovery or payment of money to a person may be enforced [on fulfilment of condition or contingency, if any (u)] by any of the usual writs of execution (v):

B., payment into Court by sequestration or (where authorised) by attachment (w):

C., recovery of land by writ of possession (x):

D., recovery of specific chattels by writ of delivery, attachment or sequestration (y).

E., an act or forbearance by attachment or committal (z), notice of the application to be served personally on the party or on his solicitor, or at his residence (a) or on a

(n) O. XLI. r. 3.
(o) Do. r. 4.
(p) Do. r. 5.
(q) Do. r. 6 ; *Perkins* v. *Dangerfield*, W. N. 1879, 172.
(r) O. XLI. A. Dec., 1879.
(s) *Attorney General* v. *Tomline*, 7 Ch. D. 388 ; *Davis* v. *Davis*, 13 Ch. D. 861.
(t) *Dann* v. *Simmins*, 40 L. J. C. P. D. 343.
(u) O. XLII. r. 7.
(v) Do. r. 1.
(w) Do. r. 2.
(x) Do. r. 3.   (y) Do. r. 4.
(z) Do. r. 5. As to what amounts to contempt, see *Edwards* v. *Edwards*, 2 Ch. D. 291 ; *In re Bryant*, 4 Ch. D. 98 ; *In re Langley*, 13 Ch. D. 110.
(a) O. XLIV. r. 2. See *Browning* v. *Sabin*, 5 Ch. D. 511 ; *In re a Solicitor*, 11 Ch. D. 152 ; *Jupp* v. *Cooper*, 5 C. P. D. 26. Similarly, in case of committal, *Richards* v. *Kitchen*, 36 L. T. 730.

clerk at his chambers (*b*).   Whether the rule as to notice applies where a *subpœna* in the Probate Division has been disregarded, *quære* (*c*).   The costs of attachment are in the discretion of the Court, and should be applied for at the time (*d*).

88. After judgment against partners, execution may issue (1) against their property as such, (2) against any person admitting on the pleadings that he is, or adjudged to be, a partner, (3) against any person served as such who has failed to appear, (4) against any person whose liability on application for leave is not disputed, or has been tried and determined (*e*).

89. Writs of execution shall be issued on production of the judgment, after a proper time has elapsed (*f*), filing of a *præcipe* signed by or on behalf of the party or his solicitor (*g*), and indorsement of the name and address of the solicitor (and principal solicitor, if any), or of the party if suing or sued in person (*h*), and the date (*i*), and further indorsement with direction to the Sheriff, &c., to levy the amount stated, and interest (if required, at four per cent., or other rate, if so agreed), and also poundage, fees, and expenses (*j*).

90. No writ shall be issued until the expiration of the time (if any) limited at or after the judgment for payment or stay of execution, but if no such time be limited, the claimant may immediately after entry of judgment sue out a writ or writs of *fi. fa.* or *elegit* (*k*).   Where a judgment has been drawn up by a Chancery Registrar for recovery of money and costs, at the election of the claimant one writ may issue, or one for recovery of the money and one for costs, the second to be not less than eight days after the first (*l*).   A writ shall remain valid

---

(*b*) *Tilney* v. *Stansfield*, W. N. 1880, 77.
(*c*) *Baigent* v. *Baigent*, 1 P. D. 421 ; *In the goods of Mary Cartwright*, 1 P. D. 422.
(*d*) *Abud* v. *Riches*, 2 Ch. D. 528.
(*e*) O. XLII. r. 8.
(*f*) Do. r. 9.
(*g*) Do. rr. 10, 10a.
(*h*) Do. r. 11.
(*i*) Do. r. 12.
(*j*) Do. rr. 13, 14.
(*k*) Do. r. 15.
(*l*) Do. r. 15a.

for one year from its issue or renewal by leave (*m*). As between the original parties it may issue within six years from judgment (*n*) in favour of or against a party or other in whose favour or against whom an Order is made (*o*), but later than six years, or after change of parties, only by leave on terms (*p*).

91. Every Order of a Court or Judge in any action, cause, or matter, may be enforced in the same way as a judgment (*q*), as *e.g.* an Order for personal payment and for foreclosure combined (*r*), a judgment on an action connected with one in another Division before the merits of this other have been determined (*s*) &c. But this does not apply to an Order dismissing an action with costs for want of prosecution (*t*).

92. Any party may apply for stay of execution or other relief on terms (*u*).

93. The Rules do not take away or curtail rights of enforcing Judgments or Orders which existed before the Judicature Acts (*v*), as *e.g.* for proceedings in Equity to obtain the benefit of a judgment (*w*).

94. Where judgment is for recovery or payment of money, an Order may be made on application (1) for oral examination of the judgment debtor as to any debts owing to him and production of books or documents (*x*), or (2) upon affidavit of the applicant or of his solicitor stating (i.) recovery of judgment, (ii.) to what amount unsatisfied, (iii.) existence of a garnishee within the jurisdiction, for attachment of all debts owing or accruing, or certainly (*y*), and not merely possibly (*z*), about to accrue from the garnishee, unless he shows cause before the

(*m*) O. XLII. r. 16.
(*n*) Do. r. 21.
(*o*) Do. r. 18.
(*p*) Do. r. 19.
(*q*) Do. r. 20.
(*r*) *Dymond* v. *Croft*, 3 Ch. D. 512.
(*s*) *Hodges* v. *Fincham*, 1 Ch. D. 9.
(*t*) *Cremetti* v. *Crom*, 4 Q. B. D. 225.
(*u*) O. XLII. r. 22.
(*v*) Do. r. 23.
(*w*) *Anglo-Italian Bank* v. *Davies*, 9 Ch. D. 275.
(*x*) O. XLV. r. 1.
(*y*) *In re Cowan's Estate*, 14 Ch. D. 638.
(*z*) *Richardson* v. *Elmit*, 2 C. P. D. 9.

Court, or a Judge, or an officer (a). But an Order dismissing with costs for want of prosecution is not a judgment under (1) (b). Joint creditors of a legatee may obtain such an Order against a receiver applied for in an administration action (c). Service of such an Order or notice to the garnishee as directed shall bind such debts in his hands (d) as against his trustee in bankruptcy (e), but an Order *nisi* does not create a charge until service (f). Where a judgment debtor neglects to comply with an examination Order under (1), application for his attachment may be made on affidavit stating (i.) that conduct money has been tendered, (ii.) that there is good reason for not examining him at his residence, (iii.) that no other means exist of ascertaining what debts are due to him (g).

95. Execution may be ordered to issue, if the garnishee does not pay into Court nor dispute his liability, or if he does not appear upon summons (h). If he does dispute his liability, it may be tried like any other issue or question in an action (i).

96. Any third person, to whom it is suggested that the garnishee debt belongs, or any lien or charge thereon as *e.g.* solicitor's lien (j), may be ordered to appear and state particulars (k); after which execution may be ordered, or any issue or question be directed to be tried, or any other such Order be made as is fit, upon terms as to a lien or charge (if any) and as to costs (l). Payment or execution shall be a valid discharge to the garnishee as against the judgment debtor, although such proceeding may be set aside (m). The costs of such attachment and incidental proceedings shall be in the discretion of the Court or

(a) O. XLV. r. 2.
(b) *Cremetti* v. *Crom*, 4 Q. B. D. 225.
(c) *In re Cowan's Estate*, 14 Ch. D. 638.
(d) O. XLV. r. 3.
(e) *Ex parte Joselyne*, 8 Ch. D. 327.
(f) *Hamer* v. *Giles*, 11 Ch. D. 942.
(g) *Protector Endowment Co.* v. *Whitham*, 36 L. T. 467.
(h) O. XLV. r. 4.
(i) Do. r. 5.
(j) *Faithfull* v. *Ewen*, 7 Ch. D. 495; *Shippey* v. *Grey*, W. N. 1880, 99.
(k) O. XLV. r. 6.
(l) Do. r. 7.
(m) Do. r. 8.

Judge (*n*). No appeal lies from a garnishee Order in a County Court, for it is not "a decision in an action or cause" within the County Court Rules, 1875 (*o*). No debt due from a corporation can be attached in the Mayor's Court by "foreign attachment" (*p*).

97. An Order charging stock or shares with immediate payment of an ascertained sum (*q*) or payment of a sum certain on a future day (*r*) may be made by any Divisional Court, not necessarily of the Division to an action in which the claimant is a party (*s*), or by any Judge, the proceedings and effect being as under 1 & 2 Vict. c. 110, ss. 14, 15, and 3 & 4 Vict. c. 82, s. 1 (*t*). But where it appears that the judgment debtor was dead when such an Order *nisi* has been made, it cannot afterwards be made absolute (*u*). A motion for such an Order, if made respecting solicitor's lien under 23 & 24 Vict. c. 127, s. 28, must be before the Judge who tried the case (*v*), and a petition by a solicitor under the same section in an action tried in a District Registry cannot be presented to a Judge in the Chancery Division (*w*), but can be if he tried the case (*x*), and should not be served on other parties (*y*).

98. Any person claiming interest in stock of any company [including the Bank of England (*z*)], may file an affidavit and notice at the Central Office, and serve copies of each on such company (*a*), to remain in force for five years (*b*), and be capable of renewal (*c*), and of withdrawal

---

(*n*) O. XLV. r. 9.
(*o*) *Mason* v. *Wirral Highway Board*, 4 Q. B. D. 459.
(*p*) *London Joint Stock Bank* v. *Aldermen of City of London*, 1 C. P. D. 1, W. N. 1880, 65.
(*q*) *Widgery* v. *Tepper* (C. A.), 6 Ch. D. 364 ; not following *Burns* v. *Irving*, 3 Ch. D. 291.
(*r*) *Bagnall* v. *Carlton*, 6 Ch. D. 130.
(*s*) *Hopewell* v. *Barnes*, 1 Ch. D. 630.
(*t*) O. XLVI. r. 1.
(*u*) *Finney* v. *Hinde*, 4 Q. B. D. 102.
(*v*) *Higgs* v. *Schrader*, 3 C. P. D. 252.
(*w*) *Owen* v. *Henshaw*, 7 Ch. D. 385.
(*x*) *Brown* v. *Trotman*, 12 Ch. D. 880.
(*y*) Do. p. 881.
(*z*) O. XLVI. r. 3.
(*a*) Do. r. 4.
(*b*) Do. r. 7.
(*c*) Do. r. 8.

by (1) written request, or (2) Order obtained on notice, or (3) petition duly served (d). But such company on receiving written request from the holder to permit the transfer of the stock, or to pay dividends, are not authorised to refuse such transfer or payment for more than eight days, without an Order of Court (e).

99. Where a person after service disobeys a judgment or ordinary four days' Order (f) for payment into Court, or doing any act in a limited time, a writ of sequestration may issue, without any Order, against his estate and effects (g), including any pension under 15 & 16 Vict. c. 54 (h). But such issue and service does not *per se* make the plaintiff a secured creditor (i). Whether a simple judgment debt can be so recovered, *quære* (j).

100. Payment of costs alone cannot be enforced by *subpœna*, nor (without leave) by sequestration (k).

(d) O. XLVI. r. 9.
(e) Do. r. 10.
(f) *Sprunt* v. *Pugh*, 7 Ch. D. 567.
(g) O. XLVII. r. 1.
(h) *Willcock* v. *Terrell*, 3 Ex. D. 323.
(i) *Ex parte Nelson, in re Hoare*, 13 Ch. D. 41.
(j) Do. pp. 45, 46, 47.
(k) O. XLVII. r. 2.

PART V.

—•—

101. Appeals to the Court of Appeal are brought by notice of motion in a summary way (*a*), and are not prevented by inrolment of decree (*b*), nor by counsel's undertaking not to appeal, unless such undertaking has been embodied in an Order (*c*). The notice shall state whether the appeal is from the whole or from what part of a Judgment or Order, including an Order of a Judge at Chambers, the appeal in this last case to be (1) on the Judge's certificate, or (2) by leave on application to set down the appeal without such certificate (*d*). There shall be fourteen days' notice of appeal from a final or interlocutory Judgment, and four days' notice from an interlocutory Order (*e*); and any doubt as to what Judgments or Orders are final and what interlocutory shall be settled by the Court of Appeal (*f*). Notice of intention to appeal may be taken as notice of appeal, *semble*, if the case is actually set down in time (*g*). The notice is to be served only on parties directly affected, unless the Court of Appeal direct service on any other parties or persons, as *e.g.*, notice of appeal by an unsuccessful defendant to be served on a successful co-defendant (*h*); notice of appeal from refusal to annul adjudication of

(*a*) O. LVIII. r. 2.
(*b*) *Hastie* v. *Hastie*, 2 Ch. D. 304.
(*c*) *Trotter's Claim*, 13 Ch. D. 261.
(*d*) *Thomas* v. *Elsom*, 6 Ch. D. 346.
(*e*) O. LVIII. r. 4.
(*f*) J. A. 1875, s. 12. Cf. *Gathercole* v. *Smith*, W. N. 1880, 102.
(*g*) *Little's Case*, 8 Ch. D. 506 ; explained in *Collins* v. *Vestry of Paddington*, 5 Q. B. D. 368.
(*h*) *Purnell* v. *Great Western Railway Co. & Harris*, 1 Q. B. D. 636.

bankruptcy to be served on the trustee (*i*), &c. The notice may be amended, by leave, as to dates or otherwise, with or without special circumstances (*j*).

102. Appeals shall be brought to the Court of Appeal by way of rehearing (*k*), and there can be no rehearing of an Order by a Judge of the High Court (*l*). An appeal cannot be reheard, nor must it be brought merely to set aside a judgment as having been obtained by fraud (*m*), nor can it raise an entirely new case, even though one supported by the old evidence (*n*). Fresh evidence may be let in (1) without special leave, on interlocutory applications, or as to matters subsequent to the decision under appeal, or (2) in other cases on special grounds in the discretion of the Court (*o*). Such evidence may be by affidavit, notice being given to the other side of application for leave to be made at the hearing (*p*). If witnesses are to be subpœnaed for oral examination at the hearing, or *semble* on deposition before an examiner, application for leave should be *previously* made by motion (*q*). Such fresh evidence may be let in, in a proper case, even where the Judge below has refused to allow it to be used to rebut a point which had taken a party by surprise at the original trial (*r*). Subject to special Order, (1) printed or office copies of affidavits on questions of fact in the Court below, (2) copies of Judge's notes, or other materials, in the discretion of the Court, as to oral evidence, shall be produced (*s*). Any party printing evidence not printed for the Court below shall bear the expense, unless before or after the printing it be otherwise ordered by the Court below, or by the Court of Appeal, or by a Judge thereof (*t*).

(*i*) *Ex parte Ward, in re Ward*, W. N. 1880, 148.
(*j*) O. LVIII. r. 3.; and see *In re Stockton Iron Furnace Co.*, 10 Ch. D. 335; *Hunter v. Hunter*, 24 W. R. 504.
(*k*) O. LVIII. r. 2.
(*l*) *In re St. Nazaire Co.*, 12 Ch. D. 88.
(*m*) *Flower v. Lloyd*, 6 Ch. D. 297.
(*n*) *Ex parte Reddish, in re Walton*, 5 Ch. D. 882.
(*o*) O. LVIII. r. 5.
(*p*) *Hastie v. Hastie*, 1 Ch. D. 562.
(*q*) *Dicks v. Brooks*, 13 Ch. D. 652. With regard to appeals to the House of Lords, fresh evidence will generally not be admitted. Per Lord Selborne: *Banco de Portugal v. Waddell*, 5 App. Cas. 170.
(*r*) *Bigsby v. Dickinson*, 4 Ch. D. 24.
(*s*) O. LVIII. r. 11.　　　　　(*t*) Do. r. 12.

103. If a respondent wishes a decision varied, whether such variation include costs or not (u) and whether as to the interest of the original appellant or not (v), he shall give to all parties affected an eight days' notice in case of appeal from a final judgment, and two days' notice from an interlocutory Order, subject to any special Order (w). Such variation must not be as to costs alone (x), but may be as to costs, charges, and expenses (y). The costs of a notice, if unsuccessful, may be ordered to be paid by the respondent (z). But though he omit such notice, the Court of Appeal has power to give any Judgment or make any Order which ought to have been made, and any further or other Order, as the case may require, as to the whole or part of a decision (whether the appeal has been made as to the whole or part) and to do so in favour of all or any of the respondents or parties (a). And the omission to appeal from any interlocutory Order or Rule shall be no bar to a decision on the merits on an appeal from the final Order (b). And the Court may set aside a (verdict and) judgment, and have a new trial, if it think there ought to be one (c). But the Court will not reverse a conclusion of fact arrived at in the Court below, except under extreme pressure, or where such conclusion depends on inferences and not merely on the credibility of witnesses (d).

104. The Court of Appeal has power to make such Order as to costs of appeal as seems just (e). The printing of shorthand notes is generally discouraged (f), and costs thereof only allowed where they are essen-

(u) *Harris* v. *Aaron*, 4 Ch. D. 749.
(v) *Ralph* v. *Carrick*, 11 Ch. D. 880.
(w) O. LVIII. rr. 6, 7 ; and see *Cracknall* v. *Janson*, 11 Ch. D. 20, and *Ex parte Payne, in re Cross*, 11 Ch. D. 539.
(x) *Harris* v. *Aaron*, 4 Ch. D. 749 ; *In re Hoskins' Trusts*, 6 Ch. D. 281 ; *Graham* v. *Campbell*, 7 Ch. D. 490.
(y) *Jones* v. *Chennell*, 8 Ch. D. 492.
(z) *The "Laurella,"* 4 P. D. 26.
(a) O. LVIII. rr. 5, 6.
(b) Do. r. 14. See *Sugden* v. *Lord St. Leonards*, 1 P. D. 208 ; *White* v. *Witt*, 5 Ch. D. 589.
(c) O. LVIII. r. 5a.
(d) *The "Glannibanta,"* 1 P. D. 283.
(e) O. LVIII. r. 5.
(f) *In re Duchess of Westminster Silver Lead Ore Co.*, 10 Ch. D. 307 ; *Kelly* v. *Byles*, 13 Ch. D. 693.

tial (*g*), and not without a special direction (*h*), nor because it has been so agreed between the solicitors (*i*), nor can costs thereof be granted after the judgment of the Court of Appeal has been drawn up (*j*). Yet they *may* sometimes be allowed even where not made for the purpose of appeal, provided they have actually been used therein (*k*). [Where one party had taken them and the other caused them to be printed, this second party was ordered to furnish printed copies to the other at a reasonable price, which price, the party furnishing being unsuccessful, was afterwards ordered to be returned (*l*).] Costs of printing *vivâ voce* evidence will be allowed where it is very voluminous and is essential to the arguing of the appeal (*m*). A successful appellant from a County Court Order in bankruptcy will generally be allowed costs (*n*). The costs of an appeal will not be deferred in order to be set off against the costs of a new trial, if successful (*o*). Costs of three Counsel *may* be allowed to the successful party in a complicated case, even though the Taxing Master had allowed only two (*p*). The Court can make no Order for costs, where the appellant has given notice but not set down the case, unless the respondent, without appearing on the appeal, makes a substantive application for his costs of the motion (*q*). Where an appeal after being set down is dismissed on the ground that notice was given too late, the appellant will not be ordered to pay costs of any affidavits filed by the respondent after the setting down (*r*).

105. The Judgment or Order appealed from or an

(*g*) *Ex parte Sawyer, in re Bowden*, 1 Ch. D. 698 ; *Lee Conservancy Board v. Button*, 12 Ch. D. 398.

(*h*) *Kirkwood v. Webster*, 9 Ch. D. 239 ; *Wells v. Mitcham Gas Co.*, 4 Ex. D. 1.

(*i*) *Ashworth v. Outram*, 9 Ch D. 483.

(*j*) *Hill's Executors v. Managers of Metropolitan Asylum District*, 49 L. J. C. L. D. 668.

(*k*) Ditto.

(*l*) *Orr, Ewing, & Co. v. Johnson & Co.*, 13 Ch. D. 450.

(*m*) *Bigsby v. Dickinson*, 4 Ch. D. 24.

(*n*) *Ex parte Masters, in re Winson*, 1 Ch. D. 113.

(*o*) *Chamberlain v. Barnwell*, W. N. 1880, 110.

(*p*) *Kirkwood v. Webster*, 9 Ch. D. 239.

(*q*) *Webb v. Mansell*, 2 Q. B. D. 117 ; *Machu v. O'Connor*, W. N. 1878, 44.

(*r*) *Ex parte Fardon's Vinegar Co.*, 14 Ch. D. 285.

office copy [unless the Order be a refusal of an interlocutory motion (s)] must be produced to, and a copy of
the notice of appeal left with, the proper officer (t), and
the appeal be set down before the day mentioned for
hearing, or, if that be in vacation, before the next day
when the Court sits; otherwise the appeal motion may
be dismissed as abandoned (u), but the respondent cannot apply to the Court for costs of this or any abandoned
appeal until he has first made a demand for payment (r).
Where an appeal is set down for hearing on a day in
vacation, it may be allowed to be heard in the following
term (w). Where an appeal is technically not set down
in time through delay of the other party in having the
Order drawn up, the respondent cannot by objecting take
advantage of his own delay (x).

106. An *ex parte* application may be made to the
Court of Appeal within four days (or time as enlarged)
from the refusal of a similar *ex parte* application by the
Court below (y). But where a Rule is asked for calling
on a Judge of a County Court to settle a case on appeal,
the Court below has discretion to grant or refuse it, and
is justified in refusing it where there plainly arises no
question of law (z).

107. Except by special leave [not granted on *ex parte*
application (a)], an appeal from an interlocutory Order,
or from an order on an interlocutory application incorpo-
rated with an Order on further consideration (b), must
be brought within twenty-one days, and any other appeal
within a year (c), the time being calculated from the date
of the signing entry, or other perfecting of the Judgment
or Order, or from the refusal of an application, refusal
with Order that the costs be costs in the cause (d), dis-

(s) *Smith* v. *Grindley*, 3 Ch. D. 80.
(t) O. LVIII. r. 8.
(u) *In re National Funds Assurance Co.*, 4 Ch. D. 303.
(r) *Griffin* v. *Allen*, 11 Ch. D 913.
(w) *Shedensack* v. *Price & Co.*, W. N. 1880, 69.
(x) *In re Hacker*, 10 Ch. D. 303.
(y) O. LVIII. r. 10.
(z) *Sharrock* v. *London & North Western Railway Co.*, 1 C. P. D. 70.
(a) *In re Lawrence. Bromett* v. *Lawrence*, 4 Ch. D. 139.
(b) *Cummins* v. *Herron*, 4 Ch. D. 787 ; *White* v. *Witt*, 5 Ch. D. 589.
(c) O. LVIII. r. 15.
(d) See *Swindell* v. *Birmingham Syndicate*, 3 Ch. D. 127.

missal of an action (e), or (in the practice of the Chancery Division) refusal to discharge a Rule made at Chambers (f), to the date of service of notice of the appeal on the respondent (g). Special leave will only be given under very special circumstances (h), and not because the Court of Appeal has subsequently construed a doubtful point of law differently, nor where the appellant was too late merely through misconstruction of time on his own part (i), or even on that of an official (j). But *semble*, leave to appeal after lapse of time will be given where there has been inevitable accident, or the other side has raised an equity against him (k). [And where notice was given but the appeal not set down in time, a second notice given within the time was held valid, the appellant offering to pay costs occasioned by the mistake (l).] Where out of several distinct claims in one application some are granted and some refused (m), or not mentioned in the Order (n), the time for an appeal on the refusal runs from the hearing. But where on petition payment is ordered of an undisputed moiety, the time for appealing on the moiety refused runs from the date of drawing up the Order (o).

108. Doubts as to what Judgments or Orders are final or interlocutory shall be determined by the Court of Appeal (p). Interlocutory Orders, so far as the time for

(e) *International Financial Society* v. *City of Moscow Gas Co.*, 7 Ch. D. 241.

(f) *Dickson* v. *Harrison*, 9 Ch. D. 243. But see *Ex parte Whittle, in re Greaves*, 49 L. J. Ch. D., where the time was said to run from the time of pronouncing the Order, not settling or signing it. In *Ex parte Ireland*, W. N. 1878, 176, the Order was not "perfected" until the date was inserted.

(g) *Ex parte Viney, in re Gilbert*, 4 Ch. D. 794 ; *Ex parte Saffery, in re Lambert*, 5 Ch. D. 365.

(h) *Craig* v. *Phillips*, 7 Ch. D. 249.

(i) *International Financial Society* v. *City of Moscow Gas Co.*, 7 Ch. D. 241. But see *Taylor's case*, 8 Ch. D. 643.

(j) *Ex parte Viney, in re Gilbert*, 4 Ch. D. 794 ; *Highton* v. *Treherne*, 46 L. J. Ex. D. 169.

(k) *McAndrew* v. *Barker*, 7 Ch. D. 705 ; *Rhodes* v. *Jenkins*, 7 Ch. D. 711.

(l) *Norton* v. *London & North Western Railway Co.*, 11 Ch. D. 118. As to extension of time for appeal after judgment on the merits, see *Collins* v. *Vestry of Paddington*, 5 Q. B. D. 368.

(m) *Traill* v. *Jackson*, 4 Ch. D. 7.

(n) *Berdan* v. *Birmingham Small Arms & Metal Co.*, 7 Ch. D. 24.

(o) *In re Michell's Trusts*, 9 Ch. D. 5.

(p) J. A. 1875, s. 12.

appealing is concerned, include Orders or Decrees in Bankruptcy, in Winding-up, or on petition for Winding-up (*q*), and in any other matter not being an action (*r*), including an Order on petition under the Trustee Relief Act (*s*), and an Order under the Vendors' and Purchasers' Act, 1874 (*t*). Also such Interlocutory Orders as finally settle the rights of parties (*tt*), so far as to fall under the twenty-one days' rule, as interpleader Orders (*u*), Orders empowering the plaintiff to sign judgment on a specially indorsed writ (*v*), discharge of a Rule for new trial (*w*), a decision of the High Court on a special case stated by an arbitrator whereon he is to make his award (*x*), and a refusal to annul an adjudication of bankruptcy (*y*). But an Order overruling a demurrer (*z*), and a judgment in an action on a replevin bond (*a*), are not interlocutory Orders; nor is an issue concerning compensation, stated under the Railways Act, 1868, a "decision made in a matter not being an action" (*b*).

109. The Court of Appeal may direct security for costs by deposit or otherwise, *e.g.* bond with sureties (*c*), under special circumstances (*d*), as *e.g.* in case of poverty of the appellant and voluminous evidence (*e*), foreign domicile and want of assets here (*f*), insolvency and vexatious prosecution (*g*), assignment of the whole property of the appellant (*h*), appeal by a company from an absolute winding-up Order, where no one else is responsible for costs (*i*), &c. Insolvency itself is *primâ facie*

(*q*) *In re National Funds Assurance Co.*, 4 Ch. D. 303.
(*r*) O. LVIII. r. 9.   (*s*) *In re Baillie's Trusts*, 4 Ch. D. 785.
(*t*) *In re Blyth & Young*, 13 Ch. D. 416.
(*tt*) See *Pheysey* v. *Pheysey*, 12 Ch. D. 305.
(*u*) *McAndrew* v. *Barker*, 7 Ch. D. 701.
(*v*) *Standard Discount Co.* v. *La Grange*, 3 C. P. D. 67.
(*w*) *Wilks, Trustees, &c.* v. *Judge*, W. N. 1880, 92.
(*x*) *Collins* v. *Vestry of Paddington*, 5 Q. B. D. 368.
(*y*) *Ex parte Ward, in re Ward*, W. N. 1880, 148.
(*z*) *Trowell* v. *Shenton*, 8 Ch. D. 318.
(*a*) *Dix* v. *Groom*, 49 L. J. C. L. 430.
(*b*) *New River Co.* v. *Midland Railway Co.*, 36 L. T. 539.
(*c*) *Phosphate Sewage Co.* v. *Hartmont*, 2 Ch. D. 811.
(*d*) O. LVIII. r. 11. See *The "Victoria,"* W. N. 1876, 145.
(*e*) *Wilson* v. *Smith*, 2 Ch. D. 67.
(*f*) *Grant* v. *Banque Franco-Egyptienne*, 2 C. P. D. 430.
(*g*) *Usil* v. *Brearley*, 3 C. P. D. 206.
(*h*) The *"Lake Megantic,"* 36 L. T. 183.
(*i*) *In re Diamond Fuel Co.*, 13 Ch. D. 412.

ground (*j*), but merely *primâ facie*, requiring extra circumstances to support it (*k*). The Court may in its discretion stay an appeal until security is given (*l*), but cannot be compelled to limit a given time under penalty of dismissing the appeal (*m*) ; but where no time is fixed in the Order, the security must be given in reasonable time according to circumstances, or the appeal will be dismissed for want of prosecution (*n*). And where additional security has been ordered, and the appellant has made delay, and only given it after notice from the respondent of motion to dismiss, the appeal cannot be heard before payment of the costs of such motion (*o*). Notice of application for security may be served without leave (*p*), and the application must be made before costs are actually incurred (*q*). These rules apply to the case of an appellant defendant (*r*) as well as plaintiff, and include appeals from the Court of the County Palatine of Lancaster (*s*).

110. No appeal shall operate as a stay of execution or of proceedings under the decision, including an injunction (*t*), except so far as may be ordered by the Court appealed from, or a Judge, or the Court of Appeal (*u*). Where the Court below has absolutely dismissed an action, it has no jurisdiction to stay proceedings pending appeal, which can only be done by injunction granted on application to the Court of Appeal (*v*). Where the defendant after decree goes into liquidation and then appeals, the Court may stay proceedings as vexatious (*w*). Such applications cannot be heard *ex parte*, but notice must be served, whether the application is made to the Court

(*j*) Per Cotton L. J. in *In re Ivory, Hankin v. Turner*, 10 Ch. D. 372.
(*k*) *Waddell v. Blockey*, 10 Ch. D. 416.
(*l*) *Clark v. Roche*, 46 L. J. 372.
(*m*) *Wilson v. Smith*, 2 Ch. D. 67.
(*n*) *Judd v. Green*, 4 Ch. D. 784 ; *Vale v. Oppert*, 5 Ch. D. 633 ; *Polini v. Gray*, 11 Ch. D. 741.
(*o*) *Ex parte Isaacs, in re Baum* (2), 10 Ch. D. 1.
(*p*) *Grills v. Dillon*, 2 Ch. D. 325.
(*q*) *Grant v. Banque Franco-Egyptienne*, 1 C. P. D. 143.
(*r*) *Dence v. Mason*, W. N. 1879, 81.
(*s*) *Lee v. Nuttall*, 12 Ch. D. 61.
(*t*) *Flower v. Lloyd*, W. N. 1877, 81.
(*u*) O. LVIII. r. 16.
(*v*) *Wilson v. Church*, 11 Ch. D. 576.
(*w*) *Vale v. Oppert*, 5 Ch. D. 969.

appealed from or to a Judge thereof (x), or if made by
motion before the Court of Appeal (y). And where any
application may be made to either Court, or to a Judge
of either, it shall be made in the first instance to the
Court or a Judge of the Court below (z), and when made
to the Court of Appeal is a motion by way of Appeal
whether formally so entered or not (a). If a party
appealing from a Judge at Chambers does not appear in
the High Court, and judgment is given against him, no
appeal lies to the Court of Appeal, but he may apply to
the Division, but *semble*, an appeal lies, if he appears,
and from some accident the case is not fully argued (b).

111. The above Rules do not affect the practice in
appeals to the House of Lords, pending which stay of
execution is obtained by giving bail in error under the
Common Law Procedure Act, 1852, s. 151, and then as
of right, and application to enlarge time for so doing
must be made to the Division of the High Court to which
the action was originally attached (c). Where the Court
of Appeal has made an Order as to costs, they may be
enforced pending appeal to the House of Lords, if the
solicitors undertake to refund them in case of reversal (d).
But where the right to appeal is unrestricted, the Court
of Appeal will ordinarily stay proceedings so far as to
prevent the appeal if successful from being nugatory (e).

112. Appeals from Inferior Courts shall be entered in
one list by the officers of the Crown Office of the Queen's
Bench Division before the day mentioned in the notice of
Appeal for the hearing (f), and they shall be heard by
such Common Law Divisional Court as shall be from
time to time directed. An appeal from a County Court
is limited to eight days, the time not to be extended (g).

(x) *Republic of Peru* v. *Weguelin*, 24 W. R. 297.
(y) O. LVIII. r. 18, O. LIII. r. 3 ; and see *Emma Silver Mining Co.* v.
Lewis, 40 L. J. C. P. D. 504.
(z) O. LVIII. r. 17.
(a) *Attorney-General* v. *Swansea Improvements & Tramways Co.*, 9 Ch. D.
16 ; explaining *Cooper* v. *Cooper*, 2 Ch. D. 492.
(b) *Walker* v. *Budden*, 5 Q. B. D. 267.
(c) *Justice* v. *Mersey Steel & Iron Co.*, 1 C. P. D. 575.
(d) *Morgan* v. *Elford*, 4 Ch. D. 352.
(e) *Polini* v. *Gray*, 12 Ch. D. 438 ; *Wilson* v. *Church*, 12 Ch. D. 454.
(f) O. LVIII. r. 19 ; and see *Donovan* v. *Brown*, 4 Ex. D. 148.
(g) *Tennant* v. *Rawlings*, 4 C. P. D. 133.

113. Costs shall be in the discretion of the Court, but trustees, mortgagees, and others shall not be thereby deprived of any costs out of particular estates or funds to which they were formerly entitled in Equity. As a rule, where an action or issue is tried by a Jury, the costs shall follow the event (*h*), whatever the amount of damages obtained (*i*), and the event is the result of all the proceedings incidental to the litigation, including a first trial (*j*), and a Rule for new trial (*k*), and the event may be distributive, where the Jury find for the plaintiff on one cause, and for the defendant on another (*l*). And costs reserved on leave to appeal, by analogy, follow the result of the appeal (*m*). But (1) where relief might have been obtained in a County Court, and the plaintiff has not recovered more than £20 on contract or £10 in tort, he shall not be entitled to any costs of the suit, unless the Judge certifies on the record that there was sufficient reason for bringing the action in the High Court (*n*); (2) the Judge may, upon or without application (*o*) upon good cause shown, at the trial, otherwise order (*p*); after the trial the Divisional Court has independent jurisdiction to deprive a successful plaintiff of costs (*q*). And where a third person opposes unsuccessfully interlocutory proceedings taken to make him a party, an Order that he pay costs is not annulled by a subsequent final judgment dismissing him from the suit, and ordering other parties to pay his costs in the cause (*r*). Where a third person is served with an Order in pursuance of a Judgment, which necessitates his appearance, he is entitled to costs of such appearance (*s*). Where an action is transferred to the

(*h*) O. LV. r. 1.
(*i*) *Parsons v. Tinling*, 2 C. P. D. 119 ; *Garnet v. Bradley*, 3 App. Cas. 944 ; *Ex parte Mercers' Co.*, 10 Ch. D. 481.
(*j*) *Field v. Great Northern Railway Co.*, 3 Ex. D. 261.
(*k*) *Creen v. Wright*, 2 C. P. D. 254.
(*l*) *Myers v. Defries*, 5 Ex. D. 15, 180.
(*m*) *Garnet v. Bradley*, 3 App. Cas. 944.
(*n*) J. A. 1873, s. 67 ; referring to County Courts Act, 1867, s. 5.
(*o*) *Turner v. Heyland*, 4 C. P. D. 432 ; *Collins v. Welch*, 5 C. P. D. 27 ; *Marsden v. Lancashire & Yorkshire Railway Co.*, 42 L. T. 630.
(*p*) O. LV. r. 1 ; and see *Harris v. Petherick*, 4 Q. B. D. 611.
(*q*) *Bowey v. Bell*, 4 Q. B. D. 95 ; *Siddons v. Lawrence*, 4 Q. B. D. 459 ; *Myers v. Defries*, 4 Ex. D. 176.
(*r*) *Beynon v. Godden*, 4 Ex. D. 246.
(*s*) *In re Orr-Ewing's Trade Marks*, W. N. 1880, 24.

High Court as being concerned with a sum exceeding £500, the plaintiff, though successful, is liable to pay costs of bringing it in the County Court (*t*). The County Court Jurisdiction Act, 1868, s. 9, is repealed as to costs by O. LV. r. 1 (*u*). Costs of an award on reference by consent (whether when compulsory, *quære*) are in the discretion of the arbitrator (*v*).

114. Security for costs may be required, among other cases, (1) where a plaintiff or counter-claiming defendant is permanently out of the jurisdiction (*w*) or goes out of it, in which latter case security may be required for past as well as future costs (*x*) ; (2) where the plaintiff becomes bankrupt or files a petition for liquidation, security may on prompt application be required for past as well as future costs (*y*) ; (3) in a second action against the same defendant for recovery of the same land (*z*) ; (4) before an Order is made under the Land Transfer Act (*a*), or the Declaration of Title Act, 1862 (*b*); (5) where the plaintiff is a Company whose assets are, on credible testimony, believed to be insufficient (*c*), as where the company is in liquidation (*d*) ; (6) where a plaintiff, having no visible means of paying, insists on bringing an action in tort in the High Court, which might have been brought in the County Court (*e*) ; (7) where a married woman (i.) sues by a next friend, who is not a person of substance (*f*), and (ii. as a general rule) where a married woman sues or defends by leave without her husband or next friend (*g*) ; (8) where an action of replevin is removed by writ of *certiorari* into the High Court at the instance of the defendant (*h*);

(*t*) *Ward v. Wyld*, 5 Ch. D. 779.
(*u*) *The " Elijah Packer*," W. N. 1877, 126.
(*v*) *Galatti v. Wakefield*, 4 Ex. D. 249.
(*w*) See *Republic of Costa Rica v. Erlanger*, 3 Ch. D. 62.
(*x*) *Massey v. Allen*, 12 Ch. D. 807.
(*y*) *Brocklebank v. King's Lynn Steamship Co.*, 3 C. P. D. 365.
(*z*) 17 & 18 Vict. c. 125, s. 93.
(*a*) 24 & 25 Vict. c. 53, s. 44.
(*b*) 24 & 25 Vict. c. 67, s. 9.
(*c*) 25 & 26 Vict. c. 89, s. 69.
(*d*) *Northampton Coal Co. v. Midland Waggon Co.*, 7 Ch. D. 500.
(*e*) 30 & 31 Vict. c. 142, s. 10, confirmed by J. A. 1873, s. 66.
(*f*) See cases collected in Daniell's Ch. Pr. 104.
(*g*) O. XV. r. 8, see para. 15.
(*h*) 19 & 20 Vict. c. 108, s. 71.

(9) under special circumstances, on appeal to the Court of Appeal (*i*); (10) on appeal to the House of Lords (*j*).

115. But no security is required of a party who resides out of the jurisdiction but comes temporarily to England to enforce a claim (*k*), or to oppose a winding-up petition (*l*). Nor where a foreigner residing abroad is for mere convenience made plaintiff in an interpleader issue (*m*). Nor where a defendant admits the plaintiff's claim, but sets up a distinct counter-claim to a larger amount, is he entitled to security as against a plaintiff residing out of the jurisdiction (*n*).

116. *Semble*, the security may be applied for in general at any time when it becomes desirable [especially where a new case has been set up materially increasing the costs (*o*)], and even though the defendant has taken some step after giving notice of his application (*p*). The amount, time, manner, and form, are in the discretion of the Court or Judge (*q*), but if in the form of a bond, it shall, unless otherwise ordered, be given to the other party, and not to an officer of the Court (*r*). Where a counter-claiming defendant residing out of the jurisdiction has to give security for general costs, this Order is not satisfied by giving security for costs of the counter-claim only (*s*).

117. Solicitors shall be entitled to costs

A. On the " Lower Scale " (*inter alia*), in cases of administration of estates under £1,000 (*t*), at the time of institution of the action; and where an equity of redemption is comprised in the estate, the value of such equity of redemption only, and not of the whole mortgaged estate, is to be estimated in the calculation of the

(*i*) O. LVIII. r. 15, see para. 109.
(*j*) St. O. IV.
(*k*) *Redondo* v. *Chaytor*, 4 Q. B. D. 453.
(*l*) *In re Percy & Kelly Nickel, Cobalt, & Chrome Iron Mining Co.*, 2 Ch. D. 531.
(*m*) *Belmonte* v. *Aynard*, 4 C. P. D. 221, 352.
(*n*) *Winterfield* v. *Bradnum*, 3 Q. B. D. 324.
(*o*) *Northampton Coal Co.* v. *Midland Waggon Co.*, 7 Ch. D. 500.
(*p*) *Arkwright* v. *Newbold*, W. N. 1880, 59.
(*q*) O. LV. r. 2.
(*r*) Do. r. 3.
(*s*) *The " Julia Fisher,"* 2 P. D. 115.
(*t*) Add. R. of Court, O. VI. 1 (1), and see *Rogers* v. *Jones*, 7 Ch. D. 345.

£1,000, subject to reduction, if on a subsequent sale its proceeds with the residue do not reach £1,000 (u).

B. On the " Higher Scale " (*inter alia*), in actions for special injunctions to restrain commission or continuance of waste (v), but only where it tends to work permanent and irreparable damage, or where title is involved, not where the damages are temporary or casual (w). But the Judge has discretion to say whether the injunction is the principal relief sought by an action (x).

The Court or Judge may allow the fees on either scale to all or either or any of the parties, as to all or any part of the costs (y), as *e.g.* where an action on a Bill of Exchange is properly brought in the Chancery Division, costs may be allowed on the higher scale (z).

118. Just and reasonable charges in procuring evidence are allowed in the Common Law as well as the Chancery Divisions (a), and may include *e.g.* surveyor's costs in an action for recovery on breach of contract (b). The Taxing Master may, with or without the direction of the Court, look into and disallow costs of statements, evidence, as affidavits (c), &c., which are improper or of unnecessary length (d). Taxed costs may be adjusted by way of deduction or set-off (e), and such right of set-off is not interfered with by solicitor's lien (f). Thus, costs due to a party on an administration suit may be set off against costs due from him on an unsuccessful motion for attachment (g). But costs in the High Court cannot be set off against costs in Bankruptcy (h). Costs of an application to extend time are, in the absence of any special Order, in the discretion of the Taxing Master (i). Where each

(u) *In re Sanderson*, 7 Ch. D. 176.
(v) O. VI. 2.
(w) *Chapman* v. *Midland Railway Co.*, 5 Q. B. D. 167, 431.
(x) *Homer* v. *Oyler*, 49 L. J. Ch. D. 655.
(y) O. VI. 3.
(z) *Pooley* v. *Driver*, 5 Ch. D. 458.
(a) Gen. Prov. 8.
(b) *Markley* v. *Chillingworth*, 2 C. P. D. 273.
(c) *Cracknall* v. *Janson*, 11 Ch. D. 1.
(d) Gen. Prov. 18.
(e) Do. 19.
(f) *Pringle* v. *Gloag*, 10 Ch. D. 676.
(g) *Robarts* v. *Buée*, 8 Ch. D. 198.
(h) *Ex parte Griffin, in re Adams*, 14 Ch. D. 37.
(i) Gen. Prov. 22a.

party succeeds on some counts, the Taxing Master may properly assign costs proportionately (*j*). Certain allowances, as, *e.g.*, refreshers (*k*) and special journey or other expenses under the head of general retainer (*l*) are within the discretion of the Taxing Master (*m*). He may disallow unnecessary or improper costs charged against a third party (*n*), as, *e.g.*, abortive garnishee summonses (*o*). The Rules of any of the old Courts, whose jurisdiction is transferred, remain in force where not inconsistent with the Acts and Rules (*p*), including the Rules of the old Court of Chancery where not altered (*q*). So, where a creditor brings an administration action on behalf of himself and other creditors, or obtains the conduct of such an action which had been originally brought by a legatee or next-of-kin, he is entitled to his costs as between solicitor and client (*r*). But, where an Order for costs is made by the Court of Appeal, the old practice does not justify any postponement of taxation without special direction (*s*). The Taxing Master may arrange what parties are to attend before him (*t*), and a solicitor has no statutory right to have the amount of his charges settled by taxation only, as, *e.g.*, against the trustee in bankruptcy (*u*). Any party dissatisfied may, before the signing of the certificate or *allocatur*, deliver to the other party, and carry in an objection in writing, specifying the items or parts objected to (*v*), and without stating the reasons for such objections (*w*); and the Taxing Master shall reconsider his taxation (*x*), and if the certificate or *allocatur* is objected to in respect of any such items

(*j*) *Knight* v. *Pursell*, 49 L. J. Ch. D. 120.
(*k*) *Harrison* v. *Wearing*, 11 Ch. D. 206.
(*l*) *In re Snell* (a solicitor), 5 Ch. D. 815.
(*m*) Gen. Prov. 29.
(*n*) Gen. Prov. 26.
(*o*) *Simmons* v. *Storer*, 14 Ch. D. 154.
(*p*) Gen. Prov. 28.
(*q*) *Pringle* v. *Gloag*, 10 Ch. D. 676.
(*r*) *In re Richardson, Richardson* v. *Richardson*, 14 Ch. D. 611.
(*s*) *Philipps* v. *Philipps*, 5 Q. B. D. 60.
(*t*) Gen. Prov. 24.
(*u*) *Ex parte Ditton, in re Woods*, 13 Ch. D. 318.
(*v*) Gen. Prov. 50.
(*w*) *Simmons* v. *Storer*, 14 Ch. D. 154.
(*x*) Gen. Prov. 31.

already objected to, such Order as may seem just may be made on application to a Judge at Chambers (y), on the original evidence, or on further evidence if directed by the Judge (z). Costs cannot ordinarily be taxed by a District Registrar (a).

119. On appeals to the House of Lords, the appellant shall give security to the Clerk of Parliaments by recognizance to the amount of £500, and sureties or payment down to the amount of £200 (b); and where any Order is made for payment of costs without specifying the amount, the Clerk of Parliaments or Clerk Assistant shall on application appoint a person to tax costs, and shall give a certificate in accordance with his report (c).

(y) In *Millard* v. *Burroughes*, W. N. 1879, 198, application by motion before Fry, J., was allowed.

(z) Gen. Prov. 32, 33.

(a) *Day* v. *Whittaker*, 6 Ch. D. 734.

(b) St. O. IV.

(c) Do. X.

PART VI.

MISCELLANEOUS.

120. An action may be transferred (1) by an Order of the Lord Chancellor to another Division with the consent of the Presidents of both Divisions, or to another Judge of the Chancery Division (*a*) ; and (2) to another Division, but not to another Judge (*b*), by an Order of Court of the original Division (*c*), or *semble*, of any Judge of any Division at Chambers (*d*), on application made on notice (*c*), with the consent of the President of the Division *to* which such action is to be transferred, but whether without the consent of the President of the Division *from* which, *quære* (*f*). Where the Judge to whom an action is assigned is absent, urgent applications will be heard by the Master of the Rolls or a Lord Justice of Appeal, on request to the Lord Chancellor, under Judicature Act, 1873, s. 51, and not under O. LI. r. 2 (*g*). In the Chancery Division, a transfer may be made of a cause to another Judge for trial or hearing only, and all other proceedings therein shall be taken as if no such transfer had been made, unless the Judge to whom such transfer for hearing is made shall direct any such proceedings to be taken before him or a Referee (*h*) ; and *semble*, the Judge who transfers a cause for hearing has no juris-

(*a*) O. LI. r. 1.
(*b*) *Chapman* v. *Real Property Trust*, 7 Ch. D. 732.
(*c*) O. LI. r. 2.
(*d*) *Hillman* v. *Mayhew*, Kelly, C. B., *dubitante*, 1 Ex. D. 132.
(*e*) *Humphreys* v. *Edwards*, 45 L. J. Ch. D. 112.
(*f*) *Storey* v. *Waddle*, 4 Q. B. D. 289.
(*g*) *Chapman* v. *Real Property Trust*, 7 Ch. D. 732.
(*h*) O. LI. r. 1a.

diction to force an interlocutory application on the hearing of the Judge to whom such cause is transferred (*i*).

121. A Judge of the Chancery Division who has made a winding-up or administration Order has power, without any further consent (*j*), on *ex parte* application (*k*), to order the transfer to himself of any action in any other Division by or against the company or representatives of the testator or intestate (*l*). So, after decree, he may transfer to his own Court an action of *devastavit* (*m*), and while an administration action is pending, he may thus transfer any action brought elsewhere against the executor *quâ* executor, but not otherwise (*n*). But where a creditor's action is thus transferred after an administration Order, it will not necessarily be stayed (*o*).

122. The Court or a Judge may, at the instance of a *defendant* (*p*), consolidate actions (*q*), and after consolidation may add new defendants (*r*); and on the application of different *plaintiffs*, may enlarge the time for the next step until one has been tried as a test-action (*s*), and where for any reason (as non-appearance of the plaintiff) such an action fails, may substitute another as a test-action (*t*).

123. Where an action has been brought on a contract, and the plaintiff's right has appeared from the pleadings, or (if none) by affidavit or otherwise, but the defendant alleges a right to be relieved from liability, an Order may be made for the preservation or *interim* custody of the subject-matter, or for bringing into Court or otherwise securing the amount in dispute (*u*). And generally, the Court or Judge may, on application by a party, make an

---

(*i*) *Lloyd* v. *Jones*, 7 Ch. D. 390.
(*j*) *In re Stubbs' Estate, Hanson* v. *Stubbs*, 8 Ch. D. 154.
(*k*) *In re Landore Siemens Steel Co.*, 10 Ch. D. 489 ; *Field* v. *Field*, W. N. 1877, 95 ; *Whittaker* v. *Robinson*, do. 201.
(*l*) O. Ll. r. 2a.
(*m*) *In re Timms*, 38 L. T. 679.
(*n*) *Chapman* v. *Mason*, 40 L. T. 678.
(*o*) *In re Timms*, W. N. 1878, 141 ; 38 L. T. 679.
(*p*) *Amos* v. *Chadwick*, 4 Ch. D. 869.
(*q*) O. Ll. r. 4.
(*r*) *In re Wortley*, 4 Ch. D. 180.
(*s*) *Amos* v. *Chadwick*, 4 Ch. D. 869 ; *Bennett* v. *Lord Bury*, 5 C. P. D. 339.
(*t*) *Robinson* v. *Chadwick*, 7 Ch. D. 878 ; *Amos* v. *Chadwick*, 9 Ch. D. 459.
(*u*) O. Ll. rr. 1, 5.

Order on terms for mandamus, injunction, or for a receiver; or otherwise for detention, preservation, or inspection of the subject-matter of the action (*v*), or for sale of any goods which it is desirable to have sold at once as being perishable, likely to be injured by keeping, or for any other just and sufficient reason (*w*). And a writ of injunction being abolished, injunction can only be obtained by Judgment or Order (*x*). A defendant may apply before judgment for injunction or for a receiver, even where the plaintiff has given notice of a similar motion, but the plaintiff himself will generally be appointed (*y*). Such jurisdiction may be exercised by the Court of Appeal even where no previous application has been made to a Divisional Court (*z*). But no such jurisdiction as to inspection may be exercised by the Masters of the Common Law Divisions (*a*).

An application (1) by the plaintiff for mandamus, injunction, or a receiver, may be *ex parte* or with notice; if for detention, preservation, or inspection, on notice to the defendant after writ of summons: (2) by any other party, after his appearance and on notice to the plaintiff (*b*). Where a specific chattel claimed in an action is retained by the other party by virtue of a lien or otherwise as security, the Court or Judge, on being satisfied by the pleadings or affidavit or otherwise, may order the property to be delivered up on payment into Court of the amount claimed in respect of such lien with or without interest and costs (*c*). But solicitor's lien does not protect any papers in the solicitor's hands from production for inspection, if ordered (*d*). And the Court may on motion during an action, or after decree for account, order an undisputed minimum (*e*), or a sum sufficiently

---

(*v*) O. LII. r. 3.
(*w*) Do. r. 2; and see *Bartholomew* v. *Freeman* (sale of a horse), 3 C. P. D. 316.
(*x*) O. LII. r. 8. For cases on injunctions and receivers see Part I. para. 6.
(*y*) *Sargant* v. *Read*, 1 Ch. D. 600.
(*z*) *Hyde* v. *Warden*, 1 Ex D. 309.
(*a*) O. LIV. r. 2, Nov., 1878.
(*b*) O. LII. r. 4.
(*c*) Do r. 6.
(*d*) *Ex parte Bramble, in re Toleman & England*, W. N. 1880, 45.
(*e*) *London Syndicate* v. *Lord*, 8 Ch. D. 84.

admitted as due by non-appearance of a party (*f*), to be paid into Court.

124. In the administration of trusts for sale, or with power of sale, the sale, unless otherwise ordered, will be given to the trustees (*g*). And where one trustee brings an action against the rest, the sale will be given by preference to them (*h*). Where it has been given to determinate persons, others (especially if parties) who interfere, as by advertising, may be stopped by injunction (*i*).

125. Applications in an action, under the Rules, to a Divisional Court or to a Judge in Court shall be by motion (*j*); and, except where expressly authorised by the Rules, shall not be for a Rule or Order to show cause (*k*). Two clear days' notice of any motion [except by special leave (*l*)] shall be given to parties affected, unless (1) where, by the previous practice, an Order or Rule has been used to be made *ex parte* absolute; (2) where otherwise provided under the present Rules; (3) where the Court or Judge, being satisfied that delay might entail serious mischief, makes an Order *ex parte* on terms, which Order the party affected may move to set aside, and the Court will not so interfere by an interlocutory Order on behalf of one party in a way which may injure the other in case he succeed in the cause itself (*m*); (4) on motion for a Rule to show cause *only* (*n*). Thus, notice must be given in case of a motion calling on a sheriff to show cause why he should not pay money levied under a *fi. fa.* (*o*), of a motion to discharge with costs a notice of appeal withdrawn by the appellant after the respondent's brief had been delivered (*p*), of a motion to send back a case to a Referee (*q*), &c. But *ex parte* application may be made for an Order *nisi* to vacate the

(*f*) *Freeman* v. *Cox*, 8 Ch. D. 148.
(*g*) O. LII. r. 6a, March, 1879.
(*h*) *In re Gardiner*, 48 L. J. Ch. D. 644.
(*i*) *Dean* v. *Wilson*, 10 Ch. D. 136.
(*j*) O. LIII. r. 1.
(*k*) Do. r. 2.
(*l*) Do. r. 4.
(*m*) *Evans* v. *Puleston*, W. N. 1880, 127.
(*n*) O. LIII. r. 3.
(*o*) *Delmar* v. *Freemantle*, 3 Ex. D. 237.
(*p*) *In re Oakwell Collieries*, 7 Ch. D. 706.
(*q*) *Grane* v. *Taylor*, 27 W. R. 412.

registration as a *lis pendens* of an action which has now been dismissed (*r*), such motion to be intituled "In the matter of 30 & 31 Vict. c. 47 and in the matter of [the action]" (*s*), for making an Order of the House of Lords an Order of the High Court (*t*), &c. And applications to assign an administration bond (*u*), and to make a Rule to pay money under an agreement of reference a rule of Court (*v*), are not motions in an action, and do not require notice. Where the party giving notice does not appear, and the party served does, the latter may be allowed costs (*w*). But if a party served has no interest (*x*), or if the notice is clearly invalid (*y*), he is not entitled to appear by Counsel merely to ask for costs.

126. A. *Without leave*, a plaintiff may serve any notice, petition, or summons on any defendant who has not appeared within the time limited (*z*).

B. *With leave*, obtained *ex parte*, he may serve notice of motion along with the writ of summons, or before the expiration of time limited for appearance (*a*).

C. The Court or a Judge may, where necessary notice has not been given, dismiss the application, or adjourn the hearing until such notice is given (*b*), and generally may adjourn the hearing of any application from time to time on terms (*c*), and also may discharge an interlocutory Order made by consent given under error on the side of one party thereto (*d*).

127. Applications at Chambers are made by summons in a summary way (*e*), and may be made before a Master in the Common Law Divisions, except such as concern (1) criminal proceedings and the liberty of the subject,

(*r*) *Pooley* v. *Bosanquet*, 7 Ch. D. 541.
(*s*) *Clutton* v. *Lee*, 7 Ch. D. 541 n.
(*t*) *British Dynamite Co.* v. *Krebs*, 11 Ch. D. 448.
(*u*) *In the goods of Mary Cartwright*, 1 P. D. 422.
(*v*) *In re Phillips* v. *Gill*, 1 Q. B. D. 78.
(*w*) *Berry* v *Exchange Trading Co.*, 1 Q. B. D. 77.
(*x*) *Campbell* v. *Holyland*, 7 Ch. D. 136.
(*y*) *Daubney* v. *Shuttleworth*, 1 Ex. D. 53.
(*z*) O. LIII r. 7.
(*a*) Do. r. 8.
(*b*) Do. r. 5.
(*c*) Do. r. 6.
(*d*) *Mullins* v. *Howell*, 11 Ch. D. 763.
(*e*) O. LIV. r. 1.

(2) transfer of actions, (3) settlement of issues not by consent, (4) discovery and inspection under O. LII. r. 3 (*f*), (5) appeals from District Registrars, (6) prohibitions, injunctions, and similar Orders, (7) awarding or reviewing taxation of costs, (8) charging Orders on stock not being Orders *nisi*, (9) acknowledgements of married women. As to interpleader:—where (1) all parties consent to a final determination without a Jury or a Special Case, and where (2) one party desires such a determination as to a sum less than £50, the question shall be determined by the Judge, unless the parties agree to refer it to the Master; in all other cases the Master has jurisdiction (*g*), A master or a District Registrar has no jurisdiction as to leave for serving a writ of summons or notice out of the jurisdiction (*h*).

128. An appeal lies from a Master *to a Judge at Chambers* by summons made returnable (*i*) within four days after the Master's decision, or further time as allowed (*j*), and such time may, under certain circumstances, be enlarged (*k*); but an appeal shall be no stay of proceedings, unless so ordered by a Judge or Master (*l*). An appeal *to the Court* in the Common Law Divisions shall be by motion on notice so made that the motion itself may be heard within eight days (*m*), or nine, if the eighth day be a Sunday (*n*), or, if no Court be meanwhile sitting, on the first day on which the Court sits after the eight days (*o*).

129. Where the facts are undisputed, questions of *law* may be stated in the form of a special case

A. by concurrence of the parties, after issue of the writ of summons (*p*).

(*f*) See para. 123.
(*g*) O. LIV. rr. 2, 2a, Nov., 1878.
(*h*) Do. r. 2b.
(*i*) *Bell* v. *North Staffordshire Railway Co.*, 4 Q. B. D. 205.
(*j*) O. LIV. r. 4.
(*k*) *Gibbons* v. *London Financial Association*, 4 C. P. D. 263.
(*l*) O. LIV. r. 5.
(*m*) *Fox* v. *Wallis*, 2 C. P. D. 45.
(*n*) *Taylor* v. *Jones*, 1 C. P. D. 87 ; and cf. O. LVII. r. 3, para. 130.
(*o*) O. LIV. r. 6 ; as amended March, 1879, subsequently to *Crom* v. *Samuels*, 2 C. P. D. 21 ; *Kuntz* v. *Sheffield*, 4 Ex. D. 150 ; *Forrest* v. *Davies*, 26 W. R. 531.   On amended Rule, see *Stirling* v. *Du Barry*, 5 Q. B. D. 65.
(*p*) O. XXXIV. r. 1.

B. by Order of the Court or Judge (q), at any stage
between appearance and trial (r); wherever it appears,
from the pleadings or otherwise, that it is convenient to
raise such question first, and to stay all proceedings
which the decision of such question may render unnecessary. Except in extreme cases, the Court of Appeal
will not interfere with a Judge's discretion in so doing (s).
And by analogy, at the trial, if it appears that the decision
of a question of law may render a question of fact unnecessary, the Court will hear the question of law first (t).
But where a married woman, infant, &c. is a party, no
special case shall be set down without leave on application, supported by evidence that the facts are true so far
as the interests of such person are concerned (u). The
parties to a special case may agree in writing on a liquidated sum payable by one to the other on judgment, with
or without costs, and enforceable by execution (v). But
no special case can be stated under 13 & 14 Vict.
c. 35 (w).

Where questions of *fact* are not sufficiently defined in
the pleadings, they may be directed to be stated in the
form of issues, to be settled, if the parties differ, by the
Judge (x).

130. In computing time, months are generally
calendar months (y); Sunday, Christmas Day, and Good
Friday, are not counted in time limited to less than six
days (z); nor Sunday or other office holiday, when by
the expiration of the time limited, any act or proceeding
cannot be done or taken on that day (a). But service of
notice (as of an appeal) is not an act which requires the
offices to be opened (b). Pleadings shall not, without
direction, be amended or delivered in the Long Vaca-

(q) Do. r. 2.
(r) *Metropolitan Board of Works* v. *New River Co.*, 2 Q. B. D. 67.
(s) Do.
(t) *Pooley* v. *Driver*, 5 Ch. D. 460.
(u) O. XXXIV. r. 4.
(v) Do. r. 6.
(w) Do. r. 7.
(x) O. XXVI.
(y) O. LVII. r. 1.
(z) Do. r. 2.
(a) Do. r. 3.
(b) *Ex parte Saffery*, *re Lambert*, 5 Ch. D. 365.

tion (c), nor shall it, without direction, be reckoned in
the time allowed for filing, amending, or delivering any
pleading (d). Service of notice or proceedings after six
o'clock shall count as on the following day, and after two
o'clock on Saturday as on the following Monday (e).

131. A. Time for delivering or amending pleadings
may be enlarged by written consent (f), or *semble*, further
enlarged (g).

B. Time for any act or proceeding may be enlarged or
abridged upon terms by a Court or Judge, even though
application is not made until after the expiration of such
time (h). But no Order can be made for leave to do one
act after another, where the Rules direct it to be done
before [*e.g.* leave to join another cause of action with an
action for recovery of land, cannot be obtained after the
issue of the writ (i)], or at the same time [*e.g.* no Order
that costs should not follow the event of a trial by a jury,
can be obtained on application to the Judge after the
trial (j)]. Nor can the time be extended for renewing a
writ, where the claim is already barred by the Statute of
Limitations (k). The Court of Appeal has original
jurisdiction to extend or abridge time (l).

132. Proceedings in a District Registry to final judgment included, shall be taken in the District Registry, in
the Books of which shall be entered (1) every final judgment and every Order for account on a defendant's
default, but except on default, a District Registrar has no
power to order account (m), (2) interlocutory judgment,
and final judgment after assessment of damages on
default of appearance or of pleading, unless otherwise
ordered by the Rules of Court or Judge (n). Actions in

(c) O. LVII. r. 4.
(d) Do. r. 5.
(e) Do. r. 8.　　　　　(f) Do. r. 6a.
(g) *King* v. *Davenport*, 4 Q. B. D. 402, was decided before the issue of r. 6a.
(h) O. LVIII. r. 6.
(i) *In re Pilcher, Pilcher* v. *Hind*, 11 Ch. D. 905.
(j) *Baker* v. *Oakes*, 2 Q. B. D. 171.
(k) *Doyle* v. *Kaufman*, 3 Q. B. D. 340.
(l) Per Jessel, M. R., in *Purnell* v. *Great Western Railway Co.*, 1 Q. B. D. 636.
(m) *Irlam* v. *Irlam*, 2 Ch. D. 608.
(n) O. XXXV. r. 1a.

the Common Law Divisions shall be entered with the Associates, *and* in the District Registry (*o*). An action in the Chancery Division commenced in a District Registry, ought to be tried in London before the Judge of the Chancery Division to whom it has been assigned (*p*). And where, by a decree of the High Court, account is ordered in a District Registry, a subsequent sale under direction of the Court may be held in London, at the Judge's discretion (*q*).

133. Writs of execution arising out of an action in a District Registry, Orders for examination of debtors for garnishee purposes, garnishee Orders, and charging Orders *nisi*, shall issue out of the District Registry, unless otherwise directed (*r*). Costs shall be taxed in a District Registry only (1) where the District Registrar has power to enter final judgment on default of the defendant (*s*), or (2) where, under special circumstances, the Court so directs (*t*). A petition by a solicitor for a charging Order *nisi* on property recovered in a trial by a jury must be presented to the Judge who tried the action, and not to the Judge of the Chancery Division to whose Court the action was attached (*u*). The District Registrar has generally the same and similarly limited authority and jurisdiction as a Master at Chambers (*v*). He cannot make an administration decree, direct accounts or inquiries (*w*), appoint a receiver, or direct banking accounts to be opened, or money to be paid into them (*x*). The rules as to applications to him, reference by him to a Judge, appeals from him, and *interim* stay of proceedings, are similar to those which govern proceedings before a Master (*y*).

134. A. Where a writ issuing out of a District Registry

(*o*) O. XXXV. r. 1b., Dec. 1879.
(*p*) *In re Smith, Hutchinson* v. *Ward,* 6 Ch. D. 692.
(*q*) *Macdonald* v. *Foster,* 6 Ch. D. 193.
(*r*) O. XXXV. rr. 3, 3a.
(*s*) Do. r. 3 ; and see *Irlam* v. *Irlam,* 2 Ch. D. 608.
(*t*) *Day* v. *Whittaker,* 6 Ch. D. 734.
(*u*) *Owen* v. *Henshaw,* 7 Ch. D. 385.
(*v*) O. XXXV. r. 5.
(*w*) *Irlam* v. *Irlam,* 2 Ch. D. 608.
(*x*) *In re Smith, Hutchinson* v. *Ward,* 6 Ch. D. 692.
(*y*) O. XXXV. rr. 5—10.

F

is specially indorsed, and the plantiff (1) has not within four days after appearance given notice of application with a view to signing final judgment, or (2) has applied, but the defendant has obtained leave to defend, and the defendant has not in either case delivered a defence, the defendant may as of right remove the action from the District Registry to London, before expiration of the time limited for defence, by delivering notice to the Registrar and service on the other parties (z).

B. Where the writ is not specially indorsed, the defendant may similarly remove the action at any time between appearance and expiration of the time limited for defence (a).

C. In any other case, any party on showing sufficient reason may apply for an order on terms (b); but if the plaintiff ought to have brought the action in the High Court on the ground that the amount exceeds £500, he may, though successful, be ordered to pay the County Court costs (c).

135. An Order on terms may be made on application by any party for sufficient reason to remove an action to a District Registry (d). But *semble*, without such Order as above, the documents may be directed to be sent up to London for the hearing, or an action may be set down in the District Registry on motion for judgment in London (e). And no further proceedings can be taken in an action commenced in a District Registry after a motion in the action has been made in the Chancery Division (f).

136. Proceedings which fail to comply with Rules of Court are not thereby avoided, unless so directed, but may be set aside as wholly or in part irregular, or amended or otherwise dealt with (g); and any defects or errors may be amended on terms, and all necessary

(z) O. XXXV. rr. 11, 12.
(a) Do. r. 11.
(b) Do. r. 13.
(c) *Ward* v. *Wyld*, 5 Ch. D. 779.
(d) O. XXXV. r. 13.
(e) See *Birmingham Waste Co.* v. *Lane*, W. N. 1876, 292; *Lumb* v. *Whiteley*, W. N. 1877, 40.
(f) *Dyson* v. *Pickles*, 27 W. R. 376.
(g) O. LIX. r. 1.

amendments made for determining the real question
at issue (*h*).

137. The Rules of the Supreme Court as to Costs,
Notices and Papers, Time, Appeals (*i*), Special Case (*j*),
Amendment (*k*), and Non-compliance (*l*), shall apply, as
far as applicable, to civil proceedings on the Crown side
of the Queen's Bench Division [including Mandamus, Quo
Warranto, and Prohibition (*m*)], and to all proceedings
on the Revenue side of the Exchequer Division (*n*): but
otherwise nothing in these Rules shall affect the procedure or practice in (1) Criminal Proceedings, (2) Proceedings on the Crown side of the Queen's Bench
Division, and (3) the Revenue side of the Exchequer
Division, and (4) proceedings for Divorce or other
Matrimonial Cause (*o*).

(*h*) O. LIX. r. 2.
(*i*) O. LXII. r. 2.
(*j*) Do. r. 3.
(*k*) Do. r. 4.
(*l*) Do. r. 5,
(*m*) Do. r. 6.
(*n*) For a case previous to these Rules of April, 1880, see *Attorney-General*
v. *Constable*, 4 Ex. D. 172.
(*o*) O. LXII. r. 1.

INDEX.

— ◆ —

ACCOUNT
    application for .
    direction for .   .   .
    indorsement on writ for .
    in District Registry   .   .

ADMINISTRATION
    of estates   .   .   .
    Order for .   .

ADMISSION
    of allegations of fact   .
    of documents .   .
    of pleadings   .   .
    Order on   .   .   .

AFFIDAVIT
    evidence on   .   .   .
    cross-examination on   .   .

AMENDMENT
    of errors   .   .
    of notice of appeal   .
    of pleadings   .

ANSWER   .
    to interrogatories   .   .

APPEAL
    to Court of Appeal   .   .
      House of Lords   .
      Privy Council   .
    from Inferior Courts   .
      County Court   .   .
      Interlocutory Order
    costs of   .   .   .
    entry of .   .   .   .
    ex parte application for   .
    notice of   .   .   .
    security for costs of .   .   .

PAGE

APPEAL—*continued.*
time for 78
variation of, by respondent 76

APPEARANCE 17, 96

ATTACHMENT
writ of 68
none by Referee 62

BANKRUPTCY
appeal from Court of 2
time for 80
jurisdiction in 2
causes no abatement 27

CAUSES OF ACTION 31

CHAMBERS
applications at, by summons 8, 93, 94

CHARGING ORDERS
how made 29, 72

CLAIM
form of pleading in statement of 33, 35
when necessary 37

COMPANIES
rules in winding up 10
Order in 90

CONSOLIDATION 90

COSTS
generally 9, 73, 83, 84
of appeal 76, 77
security for 44, 80, 84, 85
solicitors' 85, 86
taxation of 39, 86, 87, 88

COUNTERCLAIM
pleading of 30, 33, 34
when allowed 34

COUNTY COURT
appeal from 7, 72, 82
costs in 9, 84
jurisdiction of 10, 83
transfer from 10, 97, 98
to 65, 98

PAGE

DEFAULT
of appearance . . . 18
of pleading . . . 44

DEFENCE
grounds of 36, 38
pleading in statement of 33, 36
where necessary . . . 37
withdrawal of . . . 46

DEMURRER 40

DISCONTINUANCE . . . 45

DISCOVERY . . . 51, 53

DISMISSAL . . . 46

DISTRICT REGISTRY . . 58, 72, 88, 96, 97

DIVISIONS OF COURT
Chancery 1, 6, 17, 19, 47, 55, 58, 59, 60, 63, 79, 87, 89, 97, 98
Common Law . 6, 11, 17, 47, 58, 62, 67, 82, 86, 94, 93, 97

EVIDENCE
admission of . . . 64
on appeal to Court of Appeal . 75, 76, 77
to House of Lords . . 75
vivâ voce or by affidavit . . . 54

EXCHEQUER DIVISION
Revenue side of . . . 55, 99

EXECUTION
modes of . . . 68
stay of . . . 64, 70

FORMER PROCEDURE . . 11, 70

GARNISHEE . . 70, 87, 97

HOUSE OF LORDS
appeal to . . . 2, 82, 88

INDORSEMENT
of writ of summons . . . 13
special . . . 13, 19, 20, 65, 97, 98

PAGE

INFANTS
    claim by or against 24, 54
    interested in Special Case 95

INFERIOR COURTS 7, 10, 82

INJUNCTION 5. 91

INQUIRIES 54. 97

INSPECTION 52. 94
    refusal of 53

INTERLOCUTORY ORDER 11. 76
    what is 63, 79. 80

INTERPLEADER 9, 32, 80. 94

INTERROGATORIES 47
    answer to 48. 49

ISSUE OF FACT 9. 57, 59, 60, 63, 66, 95

JOINDER OF ISSUE 39, 67

JUDGMENT
    motion for 64
    entry of 65, 67
    by default 45, 65
    on admissions 40
    setting aside 68

JURISDICTION
    of Courts 1. 2, 3
    service out of 15, 94

JURY
    trial by 58, 62, 83

LEAVE TO DEFEND
    title to land 18
    on writ specially indorsed . . . 20, 98

LIQUIDATED DEMAND
    action for 12, 97, 98

LUNATICS
    claim by or against 24, 53
    interested in Special Case . . . 95

PAGE

MARRIED WOMEN
claim by or against . . — . . 23, 24
interested in Special Case . . . 95
marriage causes no abatement . . 27

MASTER
jurisdiction of . . 93, 94

MOTIONS 92, 93

NON-COMPLIANCE . 98

NOTICE
in lieu of service . . . 14, 15
to parties interested 25, 27

PARTIES
change of 27
who may be 22
third parties 17

PARTNERS
appearance of . . . 18
execution against . 69
firm of 24

PAYMENT INTO COURT 38

PETITION
evidence in support of 55

PLEADING
amendment of . 42
default of . . 44
form of . . . 35

PRIVY COUNCIL
appeal to . . . 3

PRODUCTION
what privileged from . . . 50

QUEEN'S BENCH DIVISION
Crown side of 99

QUESTIONS
of law 59, 94, 95
of fact 9, 94

PAGE

RECEIVER 5, 91, 97

RECOVERY OF LAND . . 15, 18, 19, 68, 96

REFEREE. . . . 9, 62, 65, 89

REPLY 39, 58

REPRESENTATIVE
    suing for others 23
    taking benefit of decree 28

SALE BY COURT. . . 5, 6, 7, 92

SERVICE
    of writ of execution . . 73
    of summons 14
    out of jurisdiction . . . 15, 94

SHORT CAUSE. 37

SOLICITORS
    costs of 85, 86
    lien of . . . 72
    petitions by . . . 72

SPECIAL CASE . . . 94, 95

STAY OF PROCEEDINGS
    on appeal . . . 81, 82
    on new trial . . . 64

STRIKING OUT
    interrogatories . . 48
    parties . . 26
    pleadings 43

SUMMONS
    at Chambers . . 8, 93, 94
    writ of 12

TAXATION OF COSTS . . 39, 48, 86, 87

TRANSFER OF ACTIONS
    to another Division . . 11, 89, 90
    to High Court . . 10, 97, 98

	PAGE
TIME	
for delivering pleadings . .	37, 38, 39, 40
for appeal . . .	. . 78, 79
enlargement of . . .	. . 95, 96
TRIAL.	
mode of	57
new	62
notice of	57
WRIT	
of summons . . .	. 12
of execution . . .	. 68, 97

THE END

BRADBURY, AGNEW, & CO., PRINTERS, WHITEFRIARS.

www.ingramcontent.com/pod-product-compliance
Lightning Source LLC
Chambersburg PA
CBHW030616270326
41927CB00007B/1202